NORTH WALES COAST
the story of transport
and tourism

NORTH WALES COAST
the story of transport and tourism

John Barden Davies

ISBN: 978-1-84524-182-7

Cover design: Eirian Evans

First edition: 2011
Llygad Gwalch, Ysgubor Plas, Llwyndyrys,

℡: 01758 750432

✆: llyfrau@carreg-gwalch.com
Website: www.carreg-gwalch.com

Front Cover Photograph:
The steamer *St. Tudno* arriving at Llandudno

Back Cover Photographs:
Top: Paddle steamer at Deganwy in early 20th century
Middle: Tram in Mostyn Street, Llandudno in early 20th century
Bottom: Steam train approaching Llandudno Junction in 2010

Contents

Acknowledgements	6
Preface	7
Chapter 1: Tourism, How it all began	10
Chapter 2: Early Transport and Stagecoaches	13
Chapter 3: Steamers	16
Chapter 4: Railways	24
Chapter 5: Trams	37
Chapter 6: Buses	43
Chapter 7: The Family Holiday in North Wales	69
Chapter 8: Living in a Seaside Resort	111
Chapter 9: The Decline	116
Chapter 10: Later Development and the Future	121
Appendix 1	132
Appendix 2	135
Appendix 3	137
Bibliography	139

Acknowledgements

I would like the thank the following for their help and information given in the preparation of this book.

Brian Hurst, John Glyn Jones, Ted Mack, Clive Myers, Jim Roberts, Councillor Ena Wynne, Conwy County Archives, Llandudno.

Note on copyright

Preface

I was fortunate to be born and brought up in Colwyn Bay on the North Wales coast. This was in the 1950s when there was a post-war optimism. Service personnel who returned home from military service were now bringing up their families in this new era. This was the time of the post-war baby boom and the age in which I grew up.

This book is based mainly on my own memories of those days, when visitors or holiday makers (as tourists were called in those days) came to the North Wales coast in their thousands from Lancashire, Yorkshire, and the Midlands. The more affluent would stay in hotels, but they were a minority, as most of them stayed in guest houses or even in private houses. This was the time when few people owned a car and even fewer could afford holidays abroad.

Most of the holiday makers came by train but also many by coach. This meant that intensive and varied transport systems were developed to meet their needs - trains, coaches, buses, pleasure steamers, trams. The transport systems met two needs as far as holiday makers were concerned, firstly getting the tourists to and from their destination and secondly getting them around during their stay in North Wales. They also of course met the needs of local people travelling to and from work and for their leisure travel.

Transport systems since the earliest days have responded to social and industrial needs. These systems have included horse and cart, canal boats, coastal and ocean shipping, railways, tramways, buses, cars and aircraft. It was however not until the middle of the nineteenth century that the concept of tourism and holidays and travelling for its own sake came into being.

Tourism in North Wales as elsewhere had been made possible

by social and industrial changes. Travel for the masses simply for pleasure was made available by the railways and by people having a paid holiday each year.

In North Wales, tourism has had its periods of growth and decline and probably enjoyed its heyday in the first decade of the twentieth century. Following some decline in the next two decades, tourism enjoyed a revival in the 1950s, but in reality these days were the Indian summer. Life was beginning to change and so were holiday habits. By the 1960s car ownership was increasing and cheap package holidays abroad were becoming more widely available. This meant fewer people visiting the North Wales coast for their holidays, and many were now coming for the day rather than staying. This had an effect on the many transport systems which began to decline and in addition many guest houses and hotels closed. This book gives my own recollection of those times. Although I have included some short chapters on the story and development of each of the transport systems associated with tourism in North Wales, this book is not meant to be a definitive history of the transport systems, which is already well recorded in other books. These books are listed in the biography. My knowledge of the transport systems themselves comes from my interest in them since my earliest days, most of which is recorded from my own memory. The book inevitably contains some aspects of social history as changes in holiday patterns are recorded.

The chapters on the holiday family in North Wales in the 1950s and of what it was like to live in a seaside town will I hope bring back memories to those who had holidays on the North Wales coast in those days and those who lived in the hoiday towns. Readers who remember those days will, I hope, recall with some nostalgia the seaside holidays in that period. Readers who do not remember those times will, I hope, read with interest the kind of seaside holiday their forbears enjoyed which is so different from holidays in our own time.

In a final chapter, I try to look forward to the future as things are changing again. As traffic congestion is strangling the holiday towns and petrol becomes more expensive and parking becomes difficult to find and expensive, people are beginning to realise that it can be more convenient to use public transport if a good level of service is provided. The North Wales coast now has a better and more frequent public transport system since it had in the 1950s. It is therefore not so much my intention that this book be about decline but about decline and growth and how I believe we can look forward to a new but different era of tourism in this part of the world with the transport systems of the twenty-first century responding to the rapidly changing social and industrial needs of our own day.

The main area covered in this book is what traditionally became known as the North Wales Holiday Coast; Llandudno, Colwyn Bay, Abergele, Rhyl and Prestatyn, but other parts of North Wales are included. It is principally focused on Colwyn Bay and Llandudno, as these are the towns I knew best in those days.

Although the chapters progress naturally through the history of transport systems, each chapter is complete in itself but readers will find some overlap as each transport system is related to the others. I have checked all the facts to the best of my ability, but anyone writing about times in living memory runs the risk of being corrected by others.

I dedicate this book to my late parents Alun and Peggie who were both born in Colwyn Bay and taught me so much about the area where I was born and so inspired me to write this book.

Chapter 1
TOURISM

How it all began

Two of North Wales' greatest tourist attractions, the Menai and Conwy suspension bridges serve as a reminder of the improvements in road communication in the nineteenth century. The mountainous terrain of North Wales made travel difficult and it was virtually impossible for a stagecoach to travel safely on these roads. The only alternative was to travel by sea from Liverpool to North Wales on sailing ships which was equally hazardous. As early as 1801 a group of Irish MPs demanded that action be taken to improve communication between London and Dublin. A commission was set up and determined that the port of Holyhead be used as the starting point for carrying mail and passengers to Ireland. Holyhead was already an established port. Work was started on improving the facilities of the port but when this work was complete, the problem remained of getting from London to Holyhead. The famous engineer Thomas Telford was commissioned to build two roads, one for the London to Holyhead mail coaches which would pass through Shrewsbury, Llangollen, Betws-y-coed and Bangor and another for the Chester to Bangor mail coaches which would pass through Holywell, Abergele and Conwy. By 1820 these roads were effectively complete but travellers still had to cross the river Conwy and the Menai Strait by ferry. Work then proceeded on suspension bridges and both the Conwy and Menai bridges were opened in 1826. So Telford's roads and bridges opened up North Wales to travellers.

The stagecoach, though, had its rivals. Following the first steamship, in the world *Comet* on the Clyde in 1812, the building of more steamships was soon to follow and the first passenger carrying steamship, on the North Wales coast the *Cambria* commenced sailings between Liverpool and Bagillt in Flintshire in 1821. The following year a regular steamship service was started from Liverpool to Beaumaris and Bangor. For the next thirty years, these steamships were the main link between Wales and the North of England and began calling at Llandudno and Rhyl which were then little more than small villages.

The steamers and stagecoaches carried relatively few people and the journeys still remained out of the price range of all but the most wealthy, but with the coming of the railways everything changed. When the Chester & Holyhead railway was built in 1848, people were able to travel in large numbers at relatively cheap fares. The towns of Llandudno, Rhyl and Prestatyn grew rapidly as they became popular as holiday centres. In 1865 with the selling of the Pwllycrochan estate, Colwyn Bay was born and like its neighbours on the coast grew rapidly. In response to the popularity of the railways, the steamers fought back by putting bigger and better ships on their routes and by instigating a price war. The coming of the railways meant the end of the stagecoaches.

By the beginning of the twentieth century, the towns of Llandudno, Colwyn Bay, Rhyl and Prestatyn had become established seaside resorts. Abergele, being a little inland from the sea, retained its status as a market town but the suburb of Pensarn developed as a small seaside resort. From 1858 Llandudno had its own rail link by a short branch from the main line, originally from Conwy but later at a new terminus to become known as Llandudno Junction and in 1902 a tramway was opened to carry passengers and some freight up the Great Orme. The next form of transport to be set up was an electric tram service linking Llandudno and Colwyn Bay in 1907. During the first few decades of the twentieth century motorised road traffic began to appear, both cars and buses which further aided the development of the seaside towns.

By the 1950s all these transport systems were still in operation, steamers, railways, trams and buses. They had over the past 100 years played their part in the development of all of North Wales. Although tourism is certainly the major industry in the area today, North Wales has also developed through coal and slate mining, limestone and granite quarrying, and through residential, commercial and administrative areas. The oldest industry of course is farming. But all of these industries are beyond the scope of this book, which is mainly concerned with tourism and transport.

Chapter 2
EARLY TRANSPORT AND STAGECOACHES

Until the late seventeenth and early eighteenth centuries, the only way to get around was either to walk or to travel on horseback, but not everyone had a horse. Most people never left the village where they were born. Towards the close of the seventeenth century stagecoaches were introduced. Those who travelled in them were few as the operators charged high fares. The early stagecoach journeys were both uncomfortable and dangerous. Even up to the start of the nineteenth century there were few roads that offered any degree of comfort to the stagecoach traveller. The stagecoaches themselves were primitive and those who could afford to pay a very high fare would have the privilege of sitting inside while others would have to sit on the roof being open to all weathers.

Although stagecoaches opened up travel to a small number of wealthy people, this form of transport was not without its dangers and those who travelled by such means did so at considerable risk to themselves. People who attempted a journey from either Shrewsbury or Chester to Bangor or Holyhead were in for a risky trip. The stagecoach operators faced the choice of travelling inland or travelling along the coast. There were hazards in both routes. Inland travel involved traversing mountain passes and keeping well inland of the lower reaches of the river Conwy. The coaches which travelled on the coastal route faced even greater hazards. It was reasonably easy to reach Abergele, but from there to Conwy (in those days, the next town to Abergele), was difficult. The coach had to get round Penmaen-rhos headland which in those days projected into the sea. The alternative was to turn inland at Abergele and take a much longer route to Conwy. On reaching the river Conwy, the stagecoach passengers faced more problems. They had to cross the river. The only way was to use the ferry which was unreliable and not always safe. Contemporary writers refer to the ferrymen as being ill tempered and rude. Having reached Conwy there were more problems for the traveller. At Penmaenmawr, between Conwy and Bangor the mountains literally come down into the sea, so the journey was on precipitous cliffs where many a stagecoach and its unfortunate passengers were lost into the depths. Those passengers who made it to Bangor were lucky if that was their final destination, but those bound for Ireland had more problems ahead. They had to cross the Menai Strait by ferry before they could continue their journey to Holyhead to embark on a sailing ship for Dublin. Such journeys were slow but as stagecoaches and roads improved the journey time was cut so even in those times progress was being made. Before the advent of stagecoaches, it would take up to two weeks to travel from London to Dublin, the journey being on horseback or in a small privately owned coach which was very much the preserve of the very wealthy. By the late eighteenth century the journey by public stagecoach had cut the time to about five days. By 1826 with the introduction of steam powered ferries from Holyhead to Ireland and the building of the Conwy and Menai suspension bridges, the journey time could be counted in hours rather than days. By the 1830s the journey could be completed in about 35 hours.

Another hazard for the stagecoach passengers was the danger of the coaches being attacked and the passengers robbed. The notorious highwaymen of those days put fear into all who travelled by stagecoach. As the stagecoach journeys took so long, their passengers needed somewhere to spend the night and to eat. To meet this need coaching inns were built. In one sense this can be seen as the beginning of tourism even though travel in those early days was out of necessity rather than for pleasure.

Chapter 3
STEAMERS

Stagecoaches were not without competition. The geography of the North Wales coast and its proximity to Liverpool made sea travel a viable alternative to overland stagecoach travel. Although sailing ships would have travelled between Liverpool and North Wales, it was not until the dawn of steam powered ships that sea travel became a realistic alternative. The first known passenger carrying steamship from Liverpool to North Wales began trading in 1821 between Liverpool and Bagillt in Flintshire. The following year steamships began to venture further along the coast to Bangor and Beaumaris. A steamer in the 1820s would take about five or six hours to travel from Liverpool to Bangor. This was considerably quicker than travelling by stagecoach, especially considering the stagecoach journey could involve a long wait to cross the river by ferry at Conwy. Despite the possibility of a rough passage, sea travellers were spared the uncomfortable roads and perilous journey along the edge of the cliffs at Penmaenmawr. When the Conwy and Menai suspension bridges were built and the roads were improved in 1826, the stagecoaches gained a small advantage in comfort but the steamers could still beat them in speed. Also the steamers usually had some kind of catering on board. Steamer fares were not cheap but at 10 shillings (50p) were cheaper than the stagecoaches. Sea travel, however, still carried a risk. These were small wooden paddle steamers and some of them were far from seaworthy. A number of companies competed on the Liverpool to North Wales route as there was a ready supply of passengers and there are contemporary reports of some very unpleasant passages. Matters came to a head in 1831 when a wooden paddle steamer, *Rothsay Castle*, set off from Liverpool on an August morning and at the mouth of the Mersey met a storm. The ship which had been built for short ferry services in the upper river Clyde was not suitable for the rough weather than can be experienced in the Irish Sea. The paddler struggled all day and all the following night on the passage to Beaumaris, taking in water and reducing the power of the engines. The ship was wrecked on the Dutchman's Bank at the entrance to the Menai Strait. Only 23 out of about 150 survived the wreck. New safety measures were put into effect after this and the Trwyn Du (Penmon) lighthouse was built. Following this disaster it is likely that many people returned to the stagecoaches, so the steamer companies placed better ships on the route. By the 1840s, the paddle steamers had become the principal means of travel between Liverpool and the North Wales coast, but with the coming of the railways, the role of the paddle steamers changed. Railways provided a much quicker way to get to North Wales and a price war developed between the trains and the steamers.

The golden age of the paddle steamer

It was at this time that the principal role of the paddle steamers became a means of providing excursions to North Wales from Liverpool, so we see a beginning of tourism through sea travel. The building of Llandudno Pier in 1877, to replace the old wooden pier, meant that ships could call at the landing stage at any state of the tide. A number of companies operated steamers in this period until after some amalgamations the Liverpool & North Wales Steamship Company was formed in 1891 which more or less eliminated any serious opposition, although there was some opposition for a short time in the early twenieth century by another company which offered sailings from Liverpool to Rhos-on-sea but that company went out of business after one of its steamers, the *Rhosneigr*, ran aground off Rhos Pier and was wrecked. Some remains of the wreck are still visible at exceptionally low tides. By the late nineteenth century the coastal resorts had begun to develop and piers were built providing more calling points for the steamers. In the heyday of the Liverpool and North Wales Steamship Company during the years immediately before World War 1 the company operated as many as six paddle steamers and offered a variety of sailings. The main sailing linked Liverpool with Llandudno, Beaumaris, Bangor and Menai Bridge but the company also offered local sailings along the coast serving Rhyl, Rhos-on-sea, Caernarfon and occasionally to Holyhead, Amlwch and Ynys Enlli *(Bardsey)*. Additionally a service was provided from Llandudno to Douglas Isle of Man and a sailing from Liverpool and Llandudno around the Island of Anglesey. The steamer service to Rhos-on-sea was discontinued after 1916. Also after World War 1 sailings to Rhyl were discontinued. From the mid 1920s the company began replacing its fleet of elderly paddle steamers with modern turbine ships. In 1926 the *St. Tudno*, a large ship of 2,326 tons replaced the paddler *La Marguerite*. In 1931 the *St. Seiriol*, (1,586 tons) a smaller version of the *St. Tudno* replaced the 35 year old paddler *St. Elvies*. By 1936 the modernisation of the fleet was complete with the building of the small motor ship *St. Trillo* of 314 tons to replace the paddle steamer *Snowdon*. With the passing of the paddle steamers regular sailings from Bangor, Beaumaris and Caernarfon ceased, although *St. Trillo* did make occasional calls at Beaumaris and Caernarfon and on rare occasions to Amlwch.

The three ships were requisitioned in World War 2 and *St. Seiriol* made seven crossings to Dunkirk and was in fact the first ship to arrive there in the rescue operation. *St. Seiriol* rescued many who were on other ships which had been destroyed.

Post-War revival

The ships resumed their pleasure sailings in 1946 and from then on sailings were from Liverpool to Llandudno and Menai Bridge and from Llandudno to Douglas, Isle of Man, the other ports of call having been discontinued. It is *St. Tudno*, *St. Seiriol* and *St. Trillo* that will still be remembered by older residents on the coast and holiday makers of the post war era. Many will remember some rough crossings. The *St. Tudno* was a big ship and when she was built she was the largest pleasure steamer in British waters, so why did she behave so badly in stormy weather? When in 1925 the company decided to replace the old but very popular paddle steamer *La Marguerite* described as a floating palace, it was decided to build a worthy successor that would be as popular with passengers. The new ship would be built to accommodate nearly 2500 passengers so a ship of over 2000 tons would be needed. Navigating a ship of this size through the Menai Strait at any state of the tide would be far from easy, so the answer was to ask the builders, Fairfields of Govan, Glasgow, to build a ship with as shallow a draught as possible. This was done and *St. Tudno* was built in 1926 having a tonnage of 2,326 and able to carry 2,493 passengers but with a draught of just 9 feet. This resulted in the ship rolling badly in a side wind. Also calls made at Beaumaris and Bangor had to be discontinued as the ship was too large to berth there and less easy to manoeuvre in shallow water than a paddle steamer. Although requisitioned in World War 2, *St. Tudno* was not a success due to her narrow draught and she remained in dock for most of the war. The smaller *St. Seiriol* was of better proportions and a better sea boat than *St. Tudno* having been designed for the Llandudno to Douglas service. Even so, there could be some rough passages on the *St. Seiriol*. The weather on the Irish Sea can change quickly and there were occasions when a storm blew up on the return journey from Douglas to Llandudno. The ship would make the crossing safely even if conditions were a bit lively but the problem would be berthing at Llandudno Pier. Although the pier was built in the lee of the Great Orme the landing stage was still very exposed particularly to northerly or easterly winds so it would be unsafe to berth at the pier. On such occasions the ship would anchor in Llandudno bay overnight, if it was safe to do so, or alternatively go to Liverpool from where the steamship company would have to charter a special train to return the passengers to Llandudno. On other occasions schedules would have to be changed because of the weather. Sometimes *St. Tudno* on the daily sailing from Liverpool to Llandudno and Menai Bridge would have to pass Llandudno and proceed directly to the calm Menai Strait. The small motor vessel *St. Trillo* sailed between Llandudno and Menai Bridge and also on short trips from Llandudno.

Decline in the fortunes of the steamers

These three ships were a feature of Llandudno and continued to attract large crowds of people into the early 1960s. There were times when passengers would be turned away because the ships were full to capacity. But this was the Indian summer. Soon it was all to change. A number of factors led to the demise of the Liverpool and North Wales Steamship Company. The summers of 1960-61-62 were poor with much wind and rain. The ships were getting older. There were strikes. Operating costs were rising. From 1960 the fortunes of the company declined rapidly. At the end of the 1961 season, *St. Seiriol* was laid up and the following season the Isle of Man Steam Packet took over the Llandudno to Douglas sailings using their own ships which were more modern and faster. *St. Seiriol's* half day sailings between Liverpool and Llandudno were discontinued. The 1962 season proved to be the company's last and after the end of the season the company went into liquidation. *St. Tudno* and *St. Seiriol* were sold for scrap and *St. Trillo* was bought by Townsend ferries owners of P & A Campbell who operated the ship in the Bristol Channel early and late season and in North Wales for the high season.

The Liverpool to Llandudno sailings were taken over by the Isle of Man Steam Packet operating on two or three days a week. The sailings were not extended to Menai Bridge as the ships, although not that much larger than *St. Tudno* did not have the shallow draught as did the old ship. *St. Trillo* continued to operate out of Llandudno until 1969 and Campbells showed a little more initiative that did the old company. Sailings to Caernarfon were re-introduced and also the sail round Anglesey which had last taken place in 1947 by the *St. Seiriol*.

Throughout the 1970s the sailings from Llandudno by the Isle of Man Steam Packet Company grew in popularity. Sailings to Douglas operated on up to five days a week, and the ship that had worked the sailing from Liverpool operated a cruise out of Llandudno to Point Lynas. This was immensely popular and on occasions carried in excess of 1000 passengers. By the late 1970s the Isle of Man Company was itself facing financial problems and it was no longer viable to keep ships only for the summer season, so the old passenger ships were gradually withdrawn and with them the services from Llandudno. After the 1980 season the

Liverpool-Llandudno service was withdrawn and two years later the Llandudno - Douglas service, so 1982 marked the end of regular summer passenger sailings from Llandudno.

In subsequent years the *Waverley* and *Balmoral* visited Llandudno but the *Waverley* proved unsuitable for the weather in the Irish Sea. Occasionally the *Lady of Mann* (now sold) ran a Llandudno to Douglas trip. The landing stage at Llandudno Pier has now become unusable so all that remains is an annual visit of *Balmoral* to Menai Bridge for one day for a cruise around Anglesey.

The world's first passenger hovercraft

North Wales at one time had a hovercraft service which operated from Hoylake to Rhyl in the summer of 1962. This was in fact the first passenger hovercraft service in the world. It was seen as a possible future to sea travel from Merseyside to North Wales as the conventional steamers of the day were running at a loss. Unfortunately the stormy weather of the Irish Sea meant the vessel was not able to operate the scheduled twelve crossings a day, and indeed on some days was not able to operate at all. The service only lasted for the summer of 1962 and sadly the vessel was wrecked. With just the three captains and no passengers on board, the hovercraft broke away from its moorings at Rhyl. It drifted out to sea in stormy weather and the lifeboat was soon called. The lifeboat managed to rescue the three captains, but was unable to rescue the vessel itself and had no option but to leave it to the mercy of the elements. Before too long it broke up against the sea wall at Rhyl. Whilst hovercraft have operated with success in other areas, particularly in the English Channel, the weather in the Irish Sea proved to be unsuitable for their successful commercial operation. This may well be why the Isle of Man

Steam Packet for so long resisted to use hovercraft and other high speed vessels in favour of conventional ships. It is only in comparatively modern times that high speed vessels have been a success in the Irish Sea, but even now the conventional vessels are able to withstand bad weather better.

River Sailings

Steamers plying between Liverpool and North Wales were not the only water transport provided for tourists in North Wales. For many years paddle steamers travelled from Deganwy and Conwy up the river Conwy as far as Trefriw. The reason for this was the popularity of the spa waters at Trefriw in Victorian and Edwardian times. A bath house was built in 1874 and well to do people of this era enjoyed a trip up the Conwy Valley by paddle steamer. A large hotel was built in Trefriw near to the paddle steamer landing stage. After World War 1, the spa declined in popularity and by World War 2 it had closed. However, this was not quite the end the boats sailing up the river to Trefriw. In the mid 1950s motor boat trips were being provided from Conwy to Trefriw simply for their scenic attraction and the sailing was marketed as a trip on 'the Rhine of Wales.' By the 1960s the sailings had ceased probably due to silting of the river.

In subsequent years, the spa has re-opened to the public.

Chapter 4
RAILWAYS

Tourism may have begun in a very small way with coaching inns and in a greater way with steamers, but it was the coming of the railways that made mass tourism possible at cheap fares. It was the railways that made the North Wales coast a tourist destination, indeed it was the railways which enabled the seaside resorts to develop.

Initially there was one reason for the building of the Chester to Holyhead railway, to improve communications between Dublin and London. The railway opened in 1848 from Chester to Bangor and when the tubular bridge over the Menai Strait was opened, the line was opened through to Holyhead in 1850. The line was built to get mails and passengers from London to Dublin in record time. It became possible to get from London to Dublin in 14 hours, as compared to 32 hours by the stagecoaches. This through train was named *The Irish Mail*, the oldest named train in the world. It was not long before the railway company realised the line had greater potential. Rhyl and Llandudno began to grow as a result of the railway and as early as 1858 a branch line was built to serve Llandudno. When in 1865 the Erskine family sold their estate, the town of Colwyn Bay was born and rapidly developed as it was on the rail route. Such was the popularity of the new seaside resorts that the railway line from Chester to Llandudno Junction was quadrupled in stages, the process being complete by 1915. There remained however two short sections, one between Connah's Quay and Flint and the other between Llanddulas and Colwyn Bay that remained double track. Plans to quadruple these sections never came to fruition. The other potential of railways was as carriers of heavy freight so they proved ideal for the coal and slate industries. A classic example is the town of Blaenau Ffestiniog, once with a population of 12,000 with its many slate quarries. Three railway companies saw the commercial potential of this. The first to reach the town was the Ffestiniog Railway as early as 1832 as a horse drawn railway, the horses hauling the empty wagons up from Porthmadog and the wagons returning by gravity. The trains became steam hauled from 1863. The next railway to reach Blaenau was the LNWR branch from Llandudno Junction in 1879. The line was opened in three sections, to Llanrwst in 1863, Betws-y-coed in 1867 and finally to Blaenau in 1879. The third line to reach the town was the Bala and Ffestiniog in 1882, subsequently taken over by the GWR. Although these lines were built for freight they soon started carrying passengers taking advantage of the scenic areas on their routes.

It is interesting to record that before Llandudno existed as a popular holiday town, there were other plans for the area, then known as Ormes Bay. It was to be developed as a port for the industrial output from the North Wales mines and quarries and it was intended to call it Port Wrexham. A small pier was built but was washed away in a storm so the project was abandoned and instead a town was planned as a holiday resort by the Mostyn Estates to whom much of the land in the town is still on lease.

Many branch railways were built from the Chester & Holyhead, most for freight but others for passengers. By the start of the twentieth century most places in North Wales were served by rail. In addition to the main line, branches or secondary lines were built to Mold, Denbigh, Ruthin, Corwen, Llanrwst, Betws-y-coed, Blaenau Ffestiniog, Bala, Bethesda, Gaerwen, Amlwch, Red Wharf Bay, Caernarfon, Llanberis, Nantlle, and a secondary line from Bangor and Caernarfon to join the Cambrian Coast line at Afonwen between Cricieth and Porthmadog.

The Deeside Industrial Area

The Chester to Holyhead line served three distinct areas of the coast. Firstly, the Welsh side of the Dee Estuary developed rapidly as an industrial area with a coal mine at Point of Ayr, an ironworks at Mostyn, a steel works at Shotton, and a number of chemical works around Flint and Holywell Junction (Greenfield). Mostyn and Connah's Quay developed as small ports. It was the railway which enabled these industrial complexes to develop and each one was linked to the main line by a siding. In the early twentieth century many new stations were provided to meet the needs of the many people travelling to and from work. These stations were served by stopping trains from Chester to Rhyl which called at all stations. By the mid 1960s passenger numbers had declined and with the exception of Flint, all intermediate stations between Chester and Prestatyn were closed. Later many of the industrial complexes closed and most of the freight services were withdrawn. The motive power for the freight trains in this area was provided by Mold Junction shed until it closed in 1966.

Coastal Towns and Commuter Trains

The second distinct section of the line is the holiday coast from Prestatyn to Llandudno. This area developed in a very different way from industrial Deeside. As it is recorded in other chapters of this book, this area grew as a holiday and retirement location with virtually no industry. This part of the main line enjoyed an intense service in the summer, particularly on Saturdays when the frequency of the service would do justice to a major commuter route in a large metropolis. Services in winter were much less frequent with some quite large gaps between trains. Most of the extra summer trains terminated at Llandudno, while trains which ran all the year round terminated at Bangor or Holyhead. A branch line was built from Rhyl though the Vale of Clwyd to Denbigh where it met the line from Chester to Denbigh, then continued through Ruthin to Corwen where it met the Ruabon to Barmouth line. Rhyl had a steam loco shed for these services which closed in 1963.

The coming of the railway had another effect on the development of the coastal towns in addition to tourism and retirement places. This was the development of what could certainly in the early days be called long distance commuting. Many people with businesses in Manchester and Liverpool chose to live in the North Wales coastal towns when train services made daily travel to work possible. The London & North Western Railway was quick to see the potential of running faster services for these business people and there developed what became known as 'club trains'. These were commuter trains which carried special club coaches and for an annual fee business travellers would enjoy the facilities and the privacy of a quiet coach with light refreshments and newspapers provided. In addition to the club coaches these trains carried first and second/third class coaches for the general public. Two 'club trains' ran daily from Llandudno, one to Manchester and the other to Liverpool. With the exception of the London expresses, they were by a long way the fastest trains along the North Wales coast. The locomotives used to haul them were the best engines available and the club trains were very much the principal duties of Llandudno Junction shed. Punctuality for these trains was of the utmost importance as the railway company would be required to give some compensation if the train was late arriving at its destination. This was calculated on a per minute payment for every minute of lateness. Passengers' charters have been around for some years!

The Manchester Club Train was considered the principal train of the two. Timings varied slightly over the years but a typical timing would be to leave Llandudno daily at 7.40am, after stops at Deganwy, Llandudno Junction, Colwyn Bay, Abergele, Rhyl and Prestatyn, then run non stop to Chester and after a stop at Warrington arriving in Manchester's Exchange station at about 9.55am. The return journey left Manchester at 4.30pm making the same stops and got to Llandudno by 6.45pm. The Liverpool Club train followed the Manchester one and left Llandudno at 7.50am with a similar stopping pattern to Chester except that it called additionally at Mostyn. On leaving Chester the train called at Helsby, Frodsham and Runcorn then non stop to Liverpool Lime Street where it arrived at around 10.10am. The train returned from Liverpool to North Wales at 4.30pm. The railway operated similar club trains to Manchester from Blackpool and from Windermere. The club coaches were withdrawn in World War 2 and not reinstated after the war although the timings of these commuter trains remained the same and they were still referred to by regular travellers as club trains. Even up to the early 1960s both trains carried first and second class accommodation with the Manchester train carrying a high proportion of first class coaches.

Another popular commuter train was the 7.08am Llandudno to Birkenhead Woodside although this never carried a club coach. It provided a faster option to get to Liverpool than the club train as it took a shorter route and after calling at the main stations on the coast then ran non stop from Chester to Rock Ferry. In order to get to Liverpool, passengers had the choice of changing at Rock Ferry to the underground train to Liverpool, or staying on the train and getting off at Birkenhead Woodside from where it was a short walk to the ferry boat which ran every few minutes. Passengers would be in Liverpool by just after 9am so although a change was necessary, this was for many a better option than the through Liverpool Club Train which reached Liverpool by crossing the Mersey at Runcorn. There was no through return journey from Birkenhead to Llandudno so commuters were required to travel on the return club train at 4.30pm from Liverpool which sped non stop to Chester in just 40 minutes and got to Llandudno from Liverpool in well under 2 hours. From the 1960s passengers from the North Wales coast travelling to Liverpool preferred the route via Chester and Rock Ferry as this was quicker and offered a more frequent service, even with usually two changes of train required. As a result the Liverpool Club train carried fewer passengers and by the mid 1960s had been withdrawn. The Llandudno to Birkenhead commuter train was withdrawn after Birkenhead Woodside station closed in 1967 although for a short time after this, it terminated at Rock Ferry. The timings of the old Manchester Club train, however, continued into the modern era and the train still runs to this day leaving Llandudno at 7.45 each weekday morning. It is interesting to compare the timings with the days of the old club train.

Club Train Timings

	1922	1960	1965	2010
Llandudno depart	7.52am	7.40am	7.40am	7.45am
Manchester arr	9.59am	9.59am	10.00am	9.57am
journey time	2hr 7min	2hr 19min	2hr 20min	2 hr 12min

When we compare these timings, it may seem there has been little progress but the service available today is an hourly service throughout the day from Llandudno to Manchester each train taking just over 2 hours. In 1965 there were just six through trains to Manchester from North Wales,and as it can be seen with the exception of the club train, they took much longer than the trains take today.

1965 timings on North Wales to Manchester

Holyhead	dep	....	0700	0810	....	....	1625
Bangor	dep	....	0801	0926	1210	....	1729
Llandudno	dep	0740	....	....	....	1538	....
Llan Jcn	dep	0751	0822	1005	1250	1552	1752
Manchester	arr	1000	1056	1259	1531	1835	2043
journey time							
from Llan Jcn		2.09	2.34	2.54	2.41	2.43	2.51

The Western End of the Line

The third section of the line between Llandudno Junction and Holyhead did not bring about any large scale development with the exception of Bangor and Holyhead. Bangor developed as a university city and Holyhead as a port but neither laid any claim to having developed as seaside resorts. Small stations were built in the rather remote rural area through which the line crosses Anglesey. This section had a much less frequent service, particularly between Bangor and Holyhead where most of the trains stopped at all the intermediate stations, the only exceptions being the London expresses which crossed the island non stop to Holyhead. The main express was the *Irish Mail* which ran at night all the year round and also by day in the summer. The other express which served Holyhead was the *Emerald Isle Express* which provided an early morning service to London and an early evening return. This allowed about 4 hours in London. Bangor station became an important junction with a secondary line to Caernarfon and Afonwen with connections to Pwllheli, Porthmadog and Barmouth. Also Bangor had two branch lines, one to the quarry town of Bethesda and the other to Llangefni and Amlwch on Anglesey. There was also a branch to Red Wharf Bay. An engine shed was needed at Bangor to provide the motive power for these secondary lines and also for some work on the main line. The busiest trains on the Bangor to Afonwen line were the summer only scheduled trains and specials to Butlin's Holiday Camp which effectively had its own station at Pen-y-Chain just outside Pwllheli. Apart from people going to Butlins, very few used this station. The trains which ran on Saturdays and were usually from Liverpool and Manchester were usually full and in the opinion of many, it was these trains that kept the line open. There was a similar train which approached Butlins, from the south. It commenced in Carmarthen and then traversed the very rural line through Lampeter to Aberystwyth and then up the coast through Dyfi Junction to Barmouth then on to Porthmadog and to Pen-y-Chain for Butlins. This was the only regular through train that travelled the length of the west coast of Wales. The Bangor to Afonwen line had a through train to London during the summer. This train was named, the *Welshman*. The train commenced in two sections, one at Porthmadog and the other at Pwllheli. The trains joined at Afonwen and then continued to Bangor where more coaches and a restaurant car were added. After travelling along the coast to Llandudno Junction, more coaches were added which had come from Llandudno. The train was now complete and continued its journey through Chester and Crewe to London Euston. In the 1950s and early 60s summer Saturdays saw three through trains from Pwllheli to London, each

31

on a different route. The *Welshman* as already described and also the *Cambrian Coast Express* which travelled through Harlech and Barmouth to Machynlleth and then through Newtown to Shrewsbury and onwards to London Paddington via Birmingham Snow Hill. The third route from Pwllheli to London followed the same route as the *Cambrian Coast Express* to Barmouth then turned inland through Dolgellau, Bala and Llangollen to Ruabon then to Shrewsbury then as the *Cambrian Coast Express* to Paddington. It was somewhat strange that in the timetable this train was not booked to stop at any stations between Barmouth and Ruabon, which appeared to be a lost opportunity of providing a through train from Dolgellau, Bala, Corwen and Llangollen to London. The closure of the secondary and branch lines which radiated from Bangor began as early as 1930 with the closure of the Red Wharf Bay branch. The Bethesda branch closed to passengers in 1951. When the Amlwch branch and the line to Afonwen closed in 1964, this meant the end for Bangor's steam loco shed which closed in 1965. Holyhead's loco shed lasted a little longer and eventually closed its doors in 1966. The branch from Bangor to Caernarfon survived until 1970.

Post War Revival
During the first decade of the twentieth century, the railways brought people to North Wales in large numbers, until the coming of World War 1 reduced tourism. After the war, the railways again prospered and during the 1920s and 1930s, bigger and more powerful locomotives were built which reduced journey time, together with newer ard more comfortable railway carriages. World War 2 meant a temporary end to tourism as the railways were engaged in more urgent business.

By the 1950s, the railways were enjoying a revival. I recall the times spent in those years on summer Saturday mornings watching an almost endless procession of trains through Colwyn Bay. Trains would pass as close together as the signalling system allowed with many signal boxes such as those at Nant Hall, Rhyl Sands, Llanddulas, Old Colwyn and Mochdre being open for busy times only. The trains came from numerous destinations, mostly from Manchester and Liverpool and many of the Lancashire cotton towns. There were trains from London, Cardiff, Birmingham, Staffordshire, Yorkshire and even Newcastle. Most of them were bound for Llandudno where five platforms were used, together with carriage sidings and turntable.

On an average summer Saturday more than 100 trains would pass through Colwyn Bay excluding the trains at night. It was a trainspotter's paradise.

Many of these summer Saturday trains had what we would consider today to be a bizarre stopping pattern which at a first reading of the timetable would appear to the uninitiated to be a random choice of stops. On other days, trains leaving North Wales commenced their journey at Holyhead, Bangor or Llandudno with some local stopping trains commencing at Rhyl, but on summer Saturdays the timetables of the day show how almost every station had at least one train which commenced its journey there, particularly on trains going to Manchester. One train commenced at Rhyl and then went non stop to Warrington and then some local stations to Manchester. Another began its journey at Llandudno, then picked up at Deganwy and Colwyn Bay then proceeded non stop to Chester and on to Manchester. A morning departure from Holyhead stopped at every station to Llandudno Junction where it became an express train to Chester stopping only at Rhyl. Another Manchester service commenced at Abergele and yet another at Prestatyn. The non-stop sections of these journeys brought about some impressive timings.

These are but some of what we would consider today to be a strange stopping pattern but they were for good reason. Imagine a typical summer Saturday at the stations in the coastal resorts. There was no seat reservation in those days, except on London expresses. So a train would fill up at Llandudno and by the time it got to Colwyn Bay, the large crowd of passengers waiting to board the train would not be able to get on, and the same would happen at Abergele, Rhyl and Prestatyn. For this reason the stopping patterns of the summer Saturday trains were carefully planned in the light of experience. By commencing a train at each of the main stations all the passengers could be accommodated and the trains could be got away quicker. This was of course not necessary on trains coming into North Wales and they generally stopped at all the principal stations. For example on a Manchester to Llandudno train on a summer Saturday, almost all the passengers would board at Manchester. Some trains, however did not stop at Chester and proceeded directly to North Wales. One summer Saturday train from the Birmingham area commenced its journey at Smethwick Rolfe Street rather than Birmingham New Street.

Another factor which affected the stopping patterns and routing of trains at busy times was the two sections of double track on what was otherwise quadruple from Chester to Llandudno Junction. The first one between Connah's Quay and Flint meant that few trains were able to be scheduled to stop at the intermediate stations between Chester and Prestatyn on summer Saturdays. The other double section from Llanddulas to Colwyn Bay was very much a bottleneck and for this reason not all trains stopped at Abergele. One late afternoon train from

Chester stopped at all stations to Colwyn Bay except Abergele. It then did some shunting in the yard at Colwyn Bay before taking its train as empty stock to Llandudno Junction. One of the reasons for closing Old Colwyn station as early as 1952 may well have been that it caused congestion on the double track here, particularly in summer.

At Colwyn Bay where the track reverted to quadruple as far at Llandudno Junction, trains to Holyhead were routed on the slow line and trains to Llandudno on the fast line. This is of course the opposite of what we would expect which would be for the main line trains to go on the fast line and the branch line trains on the slow line. There was however a reason for this. It meant that conflicting movements at Llandudno Junction could be avoided. There was an exception to this, however. Trains bound for Holyhead which were not required to stop at Llandudno Junction such as the *Irish Mail* were routed on the fast line at Colwyn Bay so they could pass through the Junction station at a faster speed.

From the 1960s onwards more tourists came by car and the railways carried fewer tourists. This was also the end of the steam era and the steam engine shed at Llandudno Junction closed in 1966. The quadruple track which had for so long been necessary on this busy line was no longer needed and the process of reducing it to double track had begun. With the exception of the Llandudno and Blaenau Ffestiniog lines the branches had gone, A line also remained from Bangor to Caernarfon but its days were numbered.

By the mid 1960s rail services in North Wales had been rationalised. Most services were operated by diesel multiple units with an hourly service from Bangor to Crewe and and an hourly service from Llandudno to Manchester. Between Llandudno Junction and Chester, these trains were joined together and ran as one. Some of these trains extended to Holyhead and the London to Holyhead express trains ran four times a day which remained the only loco hauled passenger trains on the coast. A lot had happened in less than ten years. By 1970 people were beginning to ask, 'Does the North Wales coast line have a future?'

Miniature Railways

Although very different from main line railways, this book would not be complete without the mention of the Marine Lake Railway in Rhyl. This 15 inch line was built in 1911 and remained popular for generations. The line was part of the Marine Lake fun fair complex but was closed in 1969 and the track was lifted. This looked like the end, but the track was re-laid and the railway re-opened in 1978 and a station was re-built in 2007. It continues to run to this day.

At Colwyn Bay, a miniature railway ran parallel to the promenade from the mid 1950s until the 1970s when the track was lifted.

Chapter 5

TRAMS

Wrexham area

Although this book is about transport systems on the North Wales holiday coast, it is relevant to mention that the first tramway system in North Wales operated in Wrexham, and not on the holiday coast until later.

Light railway systems were developed in the late nineteenth and early twentieth century. Some of the earliest were horse drawn but when electric traction was used, they soon provided a cheap way for people to travel in urban areas, particularly to work. Tramways in North Wales were by no means as numerous as they were in the industrial areas of the north of England. There were many schemes for tramways in North Wales but few came to fruition. It is not surprising that the first passenger tramway to open in North Wales was in the coal mining area around Wrexham. A horse tramway opened from Wrexham to Johnstown in 1876, but it closed in 1901. When the tramway closed, a horse bus service began on the same route which itself closed in 1903 when an electric tramway opened between Wrexham and Johnstown. This was the first electric tramway in North Wales and in an age when electricity had not yet been installed in people's homes, it is easy to imagine how impressed people were with this 'new' form of power. The intention was to run the tramway from Wrexham to the mining village of Rhosllanerchrugog, but not all the line was completed. At the Wrexham end, the terminus was, as intended, to be at the Turf Hotel by the Racecourse Football Ground which was reached, but the tramway was never to reach Rhos village itself.

It followed the route of the old horse trams as far as the village of Johnstown where a short extension was built up the hill to serve the community of Ponciau and that is as far as the tramway reached. The tramway continued an uneventful existence for the next few decades but then began to decline and eventually close. Bus services were now increasing in this busy industrial area and when the contract for the electricity supply expired in 1924, the writing was on the wall for the trams. The trams themselves were in a bad condition and services were gradually withdrawn until final closure in 1926.

Pwllheli

The next tramway to be built in North Wales was the Pwllheli & Llanbedrog in the south of the old county of Caernarfonshire. The railway reached Pwllheli in 1867 and from then on, it began to develop slowly as a resort. In the last decade of the nineteenth century a start was made on building a promenade which was some distance from the town and a horse tramway was constructed to carry the materials for building the promenade and houses.

From 1896 this tramway was opened to the public as a passenger tramway along the promenade and eventually with an extension into the town at one end and an extension to the village of Llanbedrog at the other. This popular tramway remained horse drawn for its entire life. It closed suddenly and unexpectedly when the track was washed away by a storm in 1927. The Pwllheli & Llanbedrog was run by a private operator but Pwllheli Corporation also ran their own tramway which ran from 1899 to 1919.

Llandudno and Colwyn Bay

The next two tramways to be built in North Wales are the ones that are most relevant to this book as they were both constructed on the North Wales coast. In the latter part of the nineteenth century, Llandudno was developing rapidly as a holiday resort and the developers were considering more facilities and attractions for the holiday makers. This led to the construction of a funicular tramway up to the summit of the Great Orme. This unique tramway was opened in 1902 and fortunately is still in existence. The line is in two sections with two cars operating on each section. In the centre is the machinery that drives the cars which are connected to steel cables. Originally the winding gear was powered by a steam engine but was replaced by an electric motor in the 1950s. The tram drivers and conductors communicated with the winding house by electric telegraph. The trolleys on the trams were not to pick up electricity to drive them as in a conventional tram but were the means of connecting the telephone on the tram to the winding house. By the early 1990s the wire had begun to wear out and the system was replaced by radio telephone communication. Over the years the line has been modernised and improved. It is operated by the local authority and runs during the summer months only. Despite competition from buses, cars, and the more recent cable car, the Great Orme Tramway continues to be popular with both tourists and residents alike.

Memories of holidays in Llandudno and Colwyn Bay in the 1950s will bring to mind the tramway that linked the two towns until 1956. Most tramways were built either in urban areas to link town and city centres with the suburbs or as short seaside lines usually running along promenades. The Llandudno and Colwyn Bay Electric Railway was somewhat unusual in that it was built to link two towns to each other. The main railway line along the North Wales coast which opened in 1848 was to play a major role in the development of Colwyn Bay and the branch line from Llandudno Junction opened in 1858 was in a similar way to play a major role in the development of Llandudno. The idea of a tramway to link the two towns was a progressive one as the area between the two towns was ripe for development and it would provide a more direct route than that of the railway though Llandudno Junction. The idea was born in the 1890s and a formal application made in 1897. After a number of false starts and disputes involving local authorities and landowners, it was not until November 1907 that the line eventually opened between Llandudno West Shore and the Tram Depot in Penrhyn Avenue (then known as Tramway Avenue) in Rhos-on-sea with a connecting horse bus to Colwyn Bay. By June 1908 the line was extended to Colwyn Bay. It was intended for the tracks to form a loop around Penrhyn Road and Station Road in Colwyn Bay but that never happened so by 1908 the line terminated in Abergele Road, Colwyn Bay. Despite further disputes between the tramway company and the local authorities the line was extended to the Queens Hotel in Old Colwyn in March 1915. The Llandudno terminus was at Dale Street and the intention was to extend the line to Deganwy but this was not pursued and the power was allowed to lapse and the final terminus became the West Shore at the end of Gloddaeth Avenue. As long ago as the 1920s there were signs that the tramway was facing problems as bus services were increasing and the tramcars were getting older. In 1930 the Old Colwyn section was abandoned and the eastern terminus cut back to the junction of Greenfield Road and Abergele Road in Colwyn Bay. In the 1930s the company purchased some second hand single deck cars from Accrington and also some open top double deck cars from Bournemouth. Although it appeared that the company was making progress, the fact that only second hand trams could be afforded was a sign that all was not as well as it seemed. During the Second World War, the Tramway enjoyed somewhat of a revival. This was brought about as a result of the transfer of many civil servants from London to Colwyn Bay and the fact that bus services were reduced due to fuel restrictions. In the early post war years, the Tramway was looking to the future with some optimism and it bought two enclosed double deck trams from Darwen Corporation which was closing its system. These were impressive looking vehicles and I always enjoyed travelling on them on the rare occasions they were used, usually on Saturday afternoons. They were reasonably modern and much superior to the other elderly tramcars in the fleet. It was obviously the intention of the company that these two trams should form the basis of the service from Llandudno to Colwyn Bay. However, following a Ministry of Transport inspection these vehicles were not permitted to carry passengers on Penrhyn Bay promenade, and the reserved sections on Penrhyn Hill and across Bodafon fields. This must have looked like the beginning of the end for the company, as they could only operate their two most modern vehicles for local shuttle services in Colwyn Bay and Llandudno. By the early 1950s, problems were piling up for the company as there was persistent damage to the sea wall at Penrhyn Bay, at times washing away the track. It became necessary on some occasions for passengers to have to get off one tram and walk across the gap to get on another. Eventually the seaward track at this section was abandoned and the route reduced to single track. From 1953 onwards the company began to run at a loss and consideration was being given to replacing the trams with buses. The company planned to close the line before the end of 1955, but just as various circumstances had delayed its opening half a century earlier, so circumstances delayed its closure. The Traffic Commissioners would not allow the line to close until agreement had been reached with Crosville regarding time tables. Also there were delays due to a dispute as to who would be responsible for the removal of the track. At this point it is interesting to note that much of the track remains below the road surface to this day. In the end it was the electricity company MANWEB which forced the hand of the tramway company to set a closure date. The contract was due for renewal by the summer of 1956 and MANWEB gave the company two options, either to pay them £100 a day or to install the generator at the tram depot and operate it themselves. Neither of these was a viable option, so a closure date of 24th March 1956 was quickly decided upon.

The existence of the tramway was a short one from November 1907 to March 1956, little more than 48 years, Indeed many residents of the two towns saw the beginning and end of the tramway. It did however last longer than many other tramways. It has been referred to in this chapter that the Wrexham electric tramway lasted for only 23 years. The Llandudno and Colwyn Bay Electric Railway was in fact the last surviving privately owned tramway in the UK. Indeed, there were not many corporation tramways which survived longer. The Liverpool system closed in 1957, Leeds in 1959, Sheffield in 1960 and finally Glasgow in 1962, leaving only Blackpool which runs to this day. The company ran a fleet of buses when the tram service ceased. These were old second hand buses and could not compete with Crosville who placed their newest and most comfortable buses on the route. There was much competition between the two companies but eventually the tramway company gave up the fight and sold the goodwill to Crosville for £40,000 in 1961.

Chapter 6
BUSES

Motor buses were comparative newcomers on the transport scene but their flexibility in town and country soon made them popular and tramway companies soon found they had a fierce competitor.

Crosville Motor Services

When the holiday maker of the 1950s and 60s and those who lived in the coastal towns in those days think of buses, it is always Crosville that comes to mind. For those of us who grew up on the coast, the Crosville was part of our lives. It was on a Crosville bus that we went to school. It was on a Crosville bus that our parents went to work. We went to town on a Saturday on a Crosville bus. I can remember when I was quite young returning with my parents in the car from a family holiday and the conversation started as to when we feel we are back in home territory. I can remember saying, 'I feel I am back home when I see a Crosville bus.' That sounds a strange thing to say as it was possible to see a Crosville bus anywhere between Warrington and Cardigan, but those readers who were brought up in North Wales in the 1950s and 60s will know what I mean. As I got older and beyond the age of going on holiday with my parents, it was to the Crosville I turned to find a summer job. The company employed large numbers of students during the peak holiday season of July and August. When I left home to go to university, first to Bangor and then to Lampeter, the familiar Crosville buses were there too. Most people who lived in North Wales had a member of their family who worked for Crosville or at the very least knew someone who worked for Crosville. For the holiday makers who visited the North Wales coast, particularly if they came from Merseyside and Cheshire were already familiar with Crosville at home and many of them travelled by Crosville coach to North Wales.

Crosville, although it became one of the largest bus companies started in a small way. George Crosland Taylor who originated from Yorkshire went into a partnership with a Frenchman, Georges de Ville in a car manufacturing business based in Chester in 1906. They also undertook car and boat maintenance. The name they chose for the new company was an amalgam of their own names Cros(land Taylor/ Georges de)Ville. Only five cars were ever built and they were used by family and directors. The business was not a success and soon acquired a deficit. As we would say today, a failing business often looks into diversification to improve its fortunes. This is precisely what Crosville did and saw the potential to operate a bus service between Chester and Ellesmere Port which commenced in 1911. This was ideal bus territory as the rail journey involved a roundabout route with a change at Hooton. By 1913 the company had achieved profitability and was now operating three bus services, Chester to Ellesmere Port, Chester to Kelsall and Nantwich to Crewe and Sandbach. World War 1 gave the company an opportunity to provide bus services for the workers at the munitions factory at Queensferry. This was Crosville's first venture into Wales. After World War 1 the company began to expand its services and by the mid 1920s was operating services in Liverpool which boosted their income considerably. The company had also moved further into Wales, to Mold, Ruthin and Llanrwst. Further west, Crosville by this time had reached Caernarfon and down the coast to Aberystwyth and Cardigan. In the 1920s, railway companies became concerned about competition with buses and when the 'big four' railway companies were formed in 1923, they started to think about how they could take over the bus companies. As a result, Crosville was taken over by the LMS Railway in 1929. The Crosville name was retained and the company became known as 'LMS Crosville' In 1930 there was another change. The LMS take over had not worked well and half the shares were sold to Tilling and British Automobile Traction. It was in this period that Crosville took over some important companies to consolidate their hold in North Wales. In 1930 they took over Brookes Brothers of Rhyl, Edwards of Denbigh and Silvers of Llandudno. The following year they bought out the Blues of Llandudno and Bangor. In 1933 Crosville took over Western Transport which gave them a hold in Wrexham, the largest town in North Wales, where the depot became Crosville's largest, housing more buses than their big depots in England, such as Liverpool, Rock Ferry, Chester and Crewe. Despite there having already been two takeovers, the Crosland Taylors, Claude (George Crosland Taylor's second son) and James (his third son), continued to manage the company. In 1935 Claude died and from then W.J. (as James was generally known) took over as Managing Director. By the start of World War 2, the area that had become known as Crosville territory was established and the only take overs from this period onwards were small companies. There remained some companies who retained their independence, particularly in the Wrexham area and to a lesser extent in the areas around Bangor and Caernarfon. In Llandudno and Colwyn Bay the tramway competed with Crosville but by 1961 Crosville had bought out that company, which had been a bus operator since 1956. Crosville was kept busy during World War 2, although some lesser used services were curtailed due to the shortage of fuel. During World War 2, there was yet another takeover. The Tilling Group which already owned 50% of the company took over completely and the biggest change noted by the public was the change in the livery of the buses from maroon to green. Later, the familiar look of Crosville buses was to be Bristol chasis with Eastern Coachworks bodywork, which became standard for all Tilling Group companies. In 1948 Crosville was nationalised, but still operated as a Tilling company under state ownership. In reality, things were not all that different as can be assumed by the title of W.J. Crosland Taylor's book 'State Owned with Tears' The now familiar green Bristol/ECW buses became a common sight all over North Wales. As more routes were converted to double deck operation, the Bristol Lodekka become the standard. This was one of the best buses ever built and it is the Lodekka that revives memories of people who knew the Crosville in the 1950s and 60s. The most remarkable thing about Crosville was that, despite a number of takeovers, its day to day management remained in the same family from the company's formation in 1906 until the retirement of W.J.Crosland Taylor as General Manager in 1958. It is perhaps this that gave Crosville a family feeling and a good team spirit among the company's employees. As the 1960s dawned, changes were on the horizon for Crosville and for all bus companies as private car ownership increased. Crosville had always faced problems in some of the very rural areas in which its services operated. In his book *State Owned without Tears*, Crosland Taylor devotes the whole of one appendix to this problem and predicts even as early as 1953 that the day may well come that many bus services, particularly in Wales will not be able to run unless they are subsidised. It had been Crosville policy to cross-subsidise their loss making services. Most of Crosville's profit was made in Liverpool and other centres of urban population and for many years the company was prepared to absorb the loss making services in rural areas in order to provide a service. The large profits made in the urban areas enabled them to do this. However by the 1960s it was becoming less viable to do this. In rural areas, services were never frequent so this was a greater incentive for people in these areas to buy a car, so fewer people used the buses and the losses became greater. It was in the 1960s that rural railways were beginning to close and it was Crosville who were given the task of providing rail replacement bus services. The company accepted this somewhat reluctantly and commented if there are not enough passengers to make a train service viable then how can a bus service over the same route be viable? By the mid 1960s some of the losses on the rural services had become unacceptable and many were withdrawn. In 1965, Crosville re-organised its services on the North Wales coast. Three services, Chester - Rhyl, Rhyl - Llandudno and Llandudno - Caernarfon were combined into a through Chester to Caernarfon service. One of these services was a limited stop coach which was introduced in anticipation of the closure of a number of small railway stations on the North Wales coast line. The other stopped at all bus stops between Chester and Caernarfon. At this time, many services were reduced in frequency, even in some urban areas. However, Crosville took great care, as it always had done, that connections were provided to the more rural parts of North Wales from the main towns linked by the *Cymru Coastliner* as the new limited stop service was called. Even in those days of reduction in services buses connected well and it was possible to make many connecting journeys without having to wait too long. In 1969 Crosville became part of the National Bus Company, but as on previous takeovers the Crosville name was retained.

The 1970s proved a very difficult period for Crosville and for most bus companies, but as part of the National Bus company organisation Crosville territory was extended. In Wales, some of the Western Welsh and South Wales Transport routes went over to Crosville, so Crosville buses operated as far south as Ammanford. In England some North Western Road Car services in parts of Cheshire and Lancashire went over to Crosville which in fact saw Crosville buses running into Manchester. Losses were mounting and the Crosville contacted all local authorities in its operating area with a list of all loss making services, informing the authorities that unless they provide a subsidy then these services would be withdrawn. The result was that some services were subsidised and others withdrawn. W. J. Crosland Taylor's prophetic words of 20 years previously had come true.

In 1986 the bus industry experienced its biggest change since 1930. Bus services were deregulated and state owned companies were sold off. The Government considered Crosville to be too large a company to be sold off in one, so it was split up into the Welsh and the English sections. So Crosville Cymru/Wales came into existence. The division followed the national boundaries except that Oswestry became part of Crosville Wales.

The days of cross subsidisation were well and truly over and there were many fears for the future of rural bus services. The first signs of change noticed by the public were the disappearance of most large buses and Crosville Wales began to operate minibuses even in the towns. Crosville lost many of its old established services to smaller operators. Once again an early prediction by W. J. Crosland Taylor had come true. He had said 20 years previously that many of the rural services could be better run by smaller more local companies. This proved to be the case particularly in the county of Gwynedd whose council inaugurated Bws Gwynedd for the services they subsidised and the buses had

Menai Suspension Bridge early 20th century

Entrance to Menai Suspension Bridge early 20th century.
The toll house was removed in 1940 after the bridge had been
strengthened and tolls were then abolished.

Britannia Tubular Bridge in its original state. After the fire of 1970, the bridge was re-built involving the removal of the tubes and the building of a road above the railway.

Ex-GWR Castle Class loco approaching Llandudno Junction with a steam special in August 2010. (Photo: J. B. Davies)

Ex-GWR tank loco in service on the Llangollen Railway in September 2004. (Photo: J. B. Davies)

Ffestiniog Railway loco 'Mountaineer' leaving Porthmadog in May 2004. (Photo: J. B. Davies)

Double-headed Ffestiniog Railway train leaves Porthmadog on a sunny but cold day in December 2005. (Photo: J. B. Davies)

Welsh Highland Railway Beyer-Peacock loco at Rhyd Ddu in September 2004. (Photo: J. B. Davies)

T.S. ST. SEIRIOL
1,586 Gross Tons.   Length 269 ft.   Speed 18½ knots.   1,556 Passengers.

Turbine steamer 'St Seiriol' which operated in Liverpool and North Wales from 1931 until 1961. (Postcard taken from a painting by the late John Nicholson. Author's Collection)

M.V. ST. TRILLO
314 Gross Tons.   Length 149 ft.   Speed 12 knots.   568 Passengers.

Motor vessel 'St Trillo' which operated local trips from Llandudno and Menai Bridge between 1936 and 1969. (Postcard taken from a painting by the late John Nicholson. Author's Collection)

The Pavilion was a familiar feature of Rhyl Promenade until it was demolished in the 1970s. (Author's Collection)

Old Colwyn in the 1920s. The porch of the Ship Hotel is on the right. A tram is approaching en route to Colwyn Bay and Llandudno. The trams ceased running to Old Colwyn in 1931. (Photo: Author's Collection)

Marine Hotel and Marine Terrace built in mid to late 19th century.
The terrace was purpose built as guest houses, one of which
was run by my grandmother. (Photo: Author's collection)

Colwyn Bay promenade from Old Colwyn in the 1950s.

Colwyn Bay's first Pier Pavilion built in 1900. It was destroyed by fire in 1922 and replaced by another which itself was destroyed by fire in 1934, which in turn was replaced by another. (Photo: Author's collection)

Late 1950s view of Colwyn Bay promenade and miniature railway which ran in the 1950s and 60s. The (now demolished) chalet can be seen on the right and the white house is 'Bodlondeb' a familiar landmark until demolished in the 1980s. (Photo: Author's Collection)

The site of Rhos Fynach in Rhos-on-Sea was once a monastery associated with a fishing weir. The monastery was dissolved in the 16th century but the fishing weir continued in use until World War 1. The building is now much altered and is a restaurant.
(Photo: Author's Collection)

Llandudno promenade in the late 19th/early 20th century. Note that the only form of transport visible is the horse and carriage.
(Photo: Leeds Historical Transport Society, with permission)

Llandudno Promenade in the early 20th century. The Grand Hotel on the right of the picture is still in use as a hotel today. The Pavilion in the centre of the picture, built in the 1880s was destroyed by fire in 1994.
(Photo: Author's Collection)

Tram in Mostyn Street, Llandudno in the early years of the tramway. Notice the gas lamp at the bottom of the picture.
(Photo: Author's collection)

The paddle steamer 'La Marguerite' seen here at Llandudno Pier in the early 20th century was built in 1894 for service from London to the French coast. She was popular but too expensive to operate on that route so was transferred to North Wales and from 1904 until 1925 travelled each day in the summer from Liverpool to Llandudno,

Horses and carriage taxis wait at Llandudno Pier for passengers arriving from the steamers. They didn't seem to be getting much business on this day!

Tram ascending the Great Orme in the 1950s with Llandudno Bay and the Little Orme in the background. (Photo: Author's Collection)

An already well loaded paddle steamer takes on more passengers at Deganwy. The steamer will call at Conwy before taking the passengers 12 miles up the river to the spa at Trefriw.

The inscription on the Waterloo Bridge in Betws-y-coed indicates it was so named because it was built in 1815, the year the battle of Waterloo was fought. It formed part of Telford's London to Holyhead road. The bridge still carries the A5 road today.

Diesel multiple unit train at the 'new' Blaenau Ffestiniog station in the 1980s. The train is bound for Llandudno via Betws-y-coed and Llanrwst. (Photo: J. B. Davies)

In 1965 Crosville introduced a new through limited stop coach service along the coast between Caernarfon and Chester. The journey took three and half hours, but this was still considerably quicker than the conventional bus service. (Author's Collection)

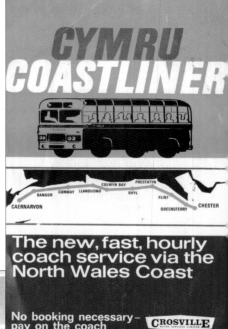

The Liverpool & N.Wales Steamship Co, published a guide to its steamer routes and the places they served. These were updated with several editions over the years of the company's existence from 1891 to 1962. This one was the last edition published. The ship featured is the 'St.Tudno'. (Author's Collection)

Preserved Leyland Tiger (KA) Crosville bus in Llandudno.
(Photo: J.B.Davies)

The square at Caernarfon (Y Maes), in the late 50s/early 60s which
was at the time the town's bus terminus. Two Crosville Bristol Lodekka
buses can be seen, one probably bound for Bangor and Llandudno.
(Photo: Author's Collection)

Late 19th/ early 20th century postcard of Pwllheli south beach.
Notice the bathing machines in the centre of the picture. In the days of
Victorian and Edwardian propriety this was the only socially acceptable
way to bathe. The machines were towed into the sea by donkeys.

Late 19th century postcard of Pwllheli south beach. It can be seen that
the town is at this time beginning to develop as a seaside resort.

a new livery with a distinctive red front. It was in this period that local authorities began to take a lead in the planning of bus services in their areas. This was indeed fortunate as without this initiative most rural bus services would have disappeared completely. Crosville Wales was bought out by its management in 1987, and then bought out by National Express in 1989. National Express sold Crosville Wales to the Drawlane company in 1991 which meant the end of the Crosville name and the services now were known as Arriva. Even today some people still refer to Arriva as Crosville. The old name hangs on in memory if not in reality.

Llandudno & Colwyn Bay Electric Railway

This company operated trams between the towns in its title between 1907 and 1956, but for the last five years of its existence was a bus company. When the tram service ceased the company bought some old second hand buses but this was not the answer to their financial problems and in 1961 the company sold out to Crosville.

Corporation Buses

The towns of North Wales never operated large fleets of buses to serve their areas, and generally services were left to Crosville and to a number of private operators who had survived being taken over by Crosville. However Llandudno UDC and the Borough of Colwyn Bay operated a seasonal bus service with small fleets of minibuses.

Colwyn Bay corporation (or UDC as it was then) began operating a summer bus service along the promenade from Old Colwyn by the railway viaduct to Rhos-on-sea, College Avenue in 1925 with a fleet of just two 20 seater buses. The preferred option was a Guy vehicle until the switch to Bedfords in 1954. Three buses would be sufficient to operate the service although the maximum fleet number was five. The buses were known by the locals as runabouts. In addition to the promenade service, a service was operated from Rhos-on-sea to Eirias Park which ascended the hill to the park from the promenade. From the early 1960s the promenade service was extended at Old Colwyn to the top of Wynnstay Road. The services were well used. When the Welsh Mountain Zoo opened in 1963 Colwyn Bay Corporation operated a free bus service to the Zoo from the Railway Station. Despite its popularity, the promenade service was discontinued in 1986 at the time of bus deregulation.

In Llandudno, a summer bus service was started by the Urban District Council in 1928 around the Marine Drive being a circular route around the Great Orme. Another route was to St. Tudno's Church on the Great Orme. These services passed to Aberconwy Council in 1974 and to Conwy County in 1996. The buses used were 20 seater Guy vehicles in the early years and Dennis vehicles in later years. These services have always been very popular and prove good value for money for the passengers especially on the Marine Drive around the Orme where a toll is charged for cars. Since 2000, this service has been operated by Alpine Travel, using re-furbished vintage coaches.

Independent Companies

Most of the independent companies providing regular bus services in the coastal towns had been taken over by Crosville in the 1930s. However, many of these companies and some newly established ones, operated coach tours and private hire services in competition with Crosville. Over the years there have been many such companies, indeed too many to mention them all by

66

name in this book. The principal companies that offered coach tours in the 1950s in the coastal towns were the Creams and the Reds in Llandudno and Pyes and Hancocks in Colwyn Bay. Many coach companies have come and gone since then but on bus deregulation in 1986 many of the independent companies began to operate bus services as well as coach tours. Today the principal independent companies operaing in and around the coastal resorts are Alpine, Express Motors, G.H.A., Menyn's, Llew Jones, M & H, Voel Coaches.

Express Coaches

In the 1950s and 60s there was an intense service of express coaches running to the coastal resorts in the summer months. Most of these were operated by Crosville and other large companies such as North Western, Ribble, Midland Red, Barton and Yelloway. Destinations served in those days from the coastal resorts were, Birkenhead, Liverpool, Runcorn, Ellesmere Port, Warrington, Wallasey, Aberystwyth, Chester, Crewe, Newcastle-under-Lyme, Sandbach, Middlewich, Wrexham, Mold, Oswestry, Llangollen, Corwen, Skipton Manchester, Birmingham, London, Nottingham. Derby, Leicester, Leeds. In the late 1960s many of the companies marketed some services together as Associated Motorways. On the formation of the National Bus Company in 1969, express services were run by National Express. Following deregulation, National Express continued as a private company and operates services from North Wales to Liverpool, Manchester, Leeds, Newcastle, Stoke, Birmingham and London.

New Innovations in Rural Areas

Bus services have always struggled in sparsely populated areas and despite many being subsidised, the buses at times run empty.

Local authorities have recently addressed this problem. Denbighshire provides what is known as 'Fflecsibus' where a small bus will take passengers to a choice of small villages as required. This has successfully avoided running empty buses on schedules to these places. Conwy Council has introduced an innovation where anyone requiring transport to and from certain villages are able to phone and then either a bus or a taxi will be provided. This service has also proved successful.

Chapter 7

THE FAMILY HOLIDAY IN NORTH WALES IN THE 1950s

In the 1950s few people had cars and holidays abroad were only for the very wealthy. Families from the North of England and the Midlands would spend their holidays in the resorts of the North Wales coast. In this chapter I shall describe what it was like for a typical family having their holiday in North Wales, how they got there, where they stayed and what they did and where they went during their holiday.

How they got to North Wales

Let us imagine it is a Saturday morning in the 1950s and we are on Colwyn Bay promenade. The beach is somewhat quieter than usual as Saturday is the 'change over day'. This is apparent as we see a seemingly endless procession of trains bringing visitors to the resorts of North Wales - an absolute paradise for trainspotters. The trains had already put down some of their passengers at Prestatyn, Rhyl and Abergele, before some more got off at Colwyn Bay, while others stayed on the train on their way to Deganwy and Llandudno.

While most came by train, others came by coach and yet others by sea from Liverpool to Llandudno. The railways were popular because they offered a luggage in advance service. The luggage would go on freight or parcels trains the previous day and would be delivered to the hotels and guest houses. This service was convenient for the visitors of course and also for the railway as it enabled them to get trains away from stations more quickly when people were not carrying luggage. However, many people still preferred to carry their own luggage.

69

The holiday family arrives at the station and soon make their way to their accommodation. Some would stay in hotels, others in less costly guest houses, but many stayed in private houses who 'took visitors.' They would get from the station by bus or even by walking if they knew the way, otherwise they would get a taxi. Sometimes people would come without having booked accommodation and would knock at doors of private houses and ask 'Do you take visitors?' In most cases the answer would be yes and the ten shillings (50p) a night which was the going rate for bed and breakfast in a private house would be a welcome supplement to the household income and good value for the holiday family. Unlike hotels or larger guest houses, the private houses that took B & B had no guest lounge and the holiday family would share the lounge with their hosts and in many cases the same families came to the same houses year after year and sometimes lifelong friendships were formed.

As well as Bed & Breakfast, other types of accommodation were available. There was 'full board' which included breakfast, lunch and dinner. This was popular with people who did not want to explore North Wales very much but just sit on the beach all day and every day of their holidays. A variation on this is what was known as 'apartments' where the holiday family would buy their own food in local shops, bring it to their hosts who would cook it for them. It is easy to imagine the chaos there must have been in guest house kitchens as different foods were being cooked for different guests! This method of catering had largely died out after World War 2, but a few guest houses still offered this until the mid 1950s. The most popular type of accommodation was Bed & Breakfast with Evening Meal. This gave the holiday makers freedom to travel to neighbouring resorts and to explore the splendid scenery of North Wales, but woe betide the family who were late for their evening meal! This was not an infrequent occurrence as there was traffic congestion even in those days. Whereas all the resorts had plenty of hotels, guest houses and private house accommodation, the areas between Rhyl and Abergele, and between Rhyl and Prestatyn provided large caravan sites which gave people the freedom of self catering. Most of these had food shops on site and a few had entertainment on site. Prestatyn had a holiday camp as early as the 1930s. It was not unknown for the residents of an entire street to holiday at the same caravan site. They would book a row of caravans so that number 1 in the street were in caravan number 1, 2 in 2 and so on. This was able to happen because of what were called Wakes Weeks, when the Lancashire cotton mill towns would each have its holiday in a particular week; one week it would be Rochdale, another week Oldham and another Burnley and so on. This also happened with people from the coal mining areas in Wales and in England. There was one more accommodation type which was popular, railway camping coaches. These were located at various locations throughout Britain, the ones in North Wales being at Abergele and Betws-y-coed. People were required to make their journey by train with a minimum number of people stipulated and could then book a camping coach at reasonable cost. They provided all the amenities of a caravan and each family had a coach to itself. Camping coaches had a distinct advantage. There was no need to get a taxi from the station as the coaches were just a few steps from the arrival platform and at Abergele the doors on the other side of the coaches opened directly on to the beach. They were convenient too for exploring North Wales by train and made good commercial sense for British Railways (as it was then), as people in these coaches would be more likely to make their trips by train rather than by coach.

Settling into the accommodation

So how is our holiday family going to spend their week? Saturday evening will usually be a walk to get their bearings and find out what there will be to do. All the transport companies would be competing for the patronage of the visitors and all issued handbills of what they had to offer. There was a choice of sea trips from Llandudno, tram rides from Llandudno and Colwyn Bay and train and coach excursions from all the resorts. The railway offered holiday runabout tickets which gave good value for unlimited travel on scheduled services throughout North Wales and also on certain excursions. British Railways gained a distinct advantage from selling these as people would use trains as their main or maybe even their only means of transport when in North Wales. It was also possible to buy a ticket which gave unlimited travel on the steamer sailings from Llandudno. Saturday evening might also be spent in a local pub where they could browse over the handbills and make plans what to do for the week. In those days pubs did not usually serve meals except those which were hotels so the holiday family would more than likely return to their guest house for an evening meal.

Some Short Trips

Sunday was a quieter day on the transport systems and most services did not get going until after lunch. The holiday family would probably not get up early and there was always a later breakfast available on Sunday. Many people would go to church while on holiday and the local churches had a greatly increased number in their congregations in the summer months. After lunch there was a choice of leisurely Sunday afternoon excursions. The railways offered a trip to Llanfairpwll in Anglesey giving tourists a 'taster' of the coastal and mountain scenery.

Afternoon tea was served on the train. For those who liked some fresh air, it was possible to take a steamer trip from Llandudno to Menai Bridge, giving an hour at the Anglesey town to walk to the bridge and back.

Let us imagine we are in the 1950s making this trip.

Memories of a steamer trip

It is a warm sunny day in June and we wait on Llandudno Pier for the departure of the *St. Tudno* for Menai Bridge. *St. Tudno* is already visible as she heads for Llandudno on the daily passage from Liverpool. As she approaches the pier at 1pm it appears she is sailing past, but no, the ship turns and berths at the pier. The ships always berthed facing the bay. Most of the passengers (probably about 700) go ashore now and will spend 4 hours in Llandudno before the ship returns to Liverpool in the evening. When all the passengers for Llandudno have disembarked we board the ship and settle down for the trip of about an hour and a quarter to Menai Bridge. The ship sounds her whistle at precisely 1.15pm, the gangways are removed and we're off. The ship turns around and heads towards the Great Orme, passing close so we have a view of the caves, only accessible by boat. As we round the Orme we see the lighthouse perched high above. As we continue we approach the Conwy estuary and pause to look up the river and see the old town of Conwy in the distance. As we continue we see the high mountains of Snowdonia coming down to meet the sea at Penmaenmawr. Looking ahead we see Puffin Island at the entrance to the Menai Strait and pass the Trwyn Du lighthouse. If we are lucky we may see some puffins and also seals. We pass through a narrow channel with the land very near as it is low tide. We turn to look at the mainland across the large sandbanks of Lafan sands towards Llanfairfechan. Before the

Menai Bridge was built cattle drovers would swim their cattle across at this point. Now the steamer is slowing down to negotiate the narrow and calm waters of the Menai Strait. Soon we pass Beaumaris, seeing clearly the green and the castle, next we pass the city of Bangor with its long pier reaching more than half way across the Strait. At one time the daily steamer from Liverpool called at Beaumaris and Bangor. Soon we see Telford's massive suspension bridge ahead and the steamer turns carefully and slowly to berth at the pier on time at 2.40pm. The weather is a little cooler now but we have an hour which gives time to walk along the promenade towards the suspension bridge and to pass under the bridge. The time soon passes and we are on board *St. Tudno* ready for the prompt departure at 3.45pm. It now starts to rain and we go below to take advantage of the facilities offered by the ship. There is a good choice, fish and chips or afternoon tea or many other foods. There are two bars with a good choice of drinks. We opt for fish and chips and a pot of tea and just finish in time for the arrival at Llandudno at 5pm. but leaving time to buy a postcard of the ship. The rain has stopped now and we get off the ship, our tickets being collected as we go and we pass the queue of people on the pier waiting to board the ship to return to Liverpool.

More short trips for Sunday afternoon

Coach companies would offer an afternoon trip to Bodnant Garden giving ample time to explore this world famous garden, have tea and be back to the guest house in time for the evening meal. Visitors to Wales in those days were surprised that pubs were not open on Sundays, so there was no Sunday evening drink in a pub. But there were ways round it. It was possible to take a short boat trip from Llandudno and there was a bar on the boat. Needless to say, this trip was very popular! Licensing laws allowed a ship's bar to serve alcohol at sea whatever the day or time. Others might accompany their hosts and be signed in at a club.

A trip to the top of Snowdon

On Monday, the holiday family would start to venture further afield and start to think of the 'must do' things on a North Wales holiday. One of these was a coach trip to the foot of Snowdon, Wales' highest mountain, and then they would travel by train to the summit. The coach journey would be a circular trip usually travelling along the coast through Conwy and Bangor to Caernarfon, where a short break was allowed for coffee, then on to Llanberis at the foot of Snowdon. The down side of this trip was that there would often be a long wait for the train at Llanberis. On a fine clear day massive queues would form and it was not unusual to have to wait two or three hours to get on the train. Families would take their turns in the queue while other family members would go to the cafe for something to eat. This situation continued for a number of years until eventually the railway company devised a better method by printing the train departure time on the tickets. There could still be a two or three hour wait but at least people no longer had to stand in a queue and families could go to a cafe and have a meal together during the waiting time. Everyone who makes this trip, particularly on a clear day agrees it is well worth the wait for a ride on this unique railway amidst spectaculour scenery.

After the trip up the mountain, passengers would re-join the coach to cross the spectaculour Llanberis Pass through the heart of Snowdonia, and then continue through the mountain village of Capel Curig and the popular resort of Betws-y-coed, where if time allowed there would be a stop for tea.

Across the sea to the Isle of Man

On Tuesday the holiday family would do another 'must do' trip, a steamer sailing from Llandudno to the Isle of Man aboard the Liverpool & North Wales Steamship Company's *St. Seiriol*. The steamer took about three and half hours to cross to the island and most of the passengers would have lunch on the ship to enable them to have more time in Douglas. On arrival at Douglas, passengers would have just under three hours on the island. Coach trips were available for those wanting to explore the island. The weather in the Irish Sea can change quickly and this made the return trip somewhat unpredictable. In easterly gales, it was difficult and sometimes impossible for ships to sail into or out of Douglas harbour. On such occasions *St. Seiriol* would remain in the harbour overnight with passengers being given the choice of staying in a hotel or sleeping on the ship, but they were spared a rough crossing. On occasions when there was rough weather from the north, west or south, the steamer would leave Douglas and her passengers would have a very rough crossing indeed. The sight of Llandudno was like an oasis in a desert, but often hopes would soon be disappointed as the weather was too bad for the ship to berth at the pier. The ship's captain then faced a choice; either to anchor in Llandudno bay until the storm abated, but if the wind was blowing towards the shore this could be dangerous, so the alternative was to make for the Mersey and land the passengers at Liverpool. The steamship company would then have to put on a special train at short notice to get the passengers back to North Wales. Such rough crossings would happen now and again but more often than not this was a pleasant trip which was very popular with visitors and locals alike.

Around North Wales by land cruise train

After having sampled a coach trip and a steamer trip the holiday family might well take an all day train trip on Wednesday. This may well be on the *North Wales Land Cruise* or *Cambrian Radio Cruise*. This was a circular trip of coast, valleys, lakes and mountains. There were four starting points for trains on this route but let us follow the holiday family as they make their journey from Llandudno. We settle down in a comfortable train with a table at every seat. As soon as the train leaves Llandudno we see the panorama of the Conwy estuary and in the distance the island of Anglesey and Puffin Island. The train now picks up some passengers at Deganwy and from here we have a view across the river to Conwy dominated by its castle. After a stop at Llandudno Junction the train turns inland for four miles until it rejoins the sea at Colwyn Bay where more passengers get on. The train then follows the coast and after a call at Abergele takes on a large number of passengers at Rhyl. As we leave Rhyl station, coffee and refreshments are brought to our table and the loudspeaker system comes into action with a commentary on the passing scenery. So soon after leaving Rhyl's buslting station we are in a different world as we take the branch line up the Vale of Clwyd, passing through St. Asaph with its cathedral, then on through the ancient market towns of Denbigh and Ruthin. This is farming country and we relax as we look at this green and peaceful valley. After leaving Ruthin we continue through the upper Clwyd valley passing through Eyarth gorge where railway, road and river are in close proximity through this narrow part of the valley. From here the train moves on to Corwen in the Dee Valley to join the Ruabon to Barmouth line. From Corwen we proceed through more farmland to Bala as this very rural route runs by the side of Llyn Tegid (Bala Lake), at about five miles long, this is Wales' largest natural lake. As we pass through Llanuwchllyn at the head of the lake the scenery begins to get more mountainous as we cross the summit of the line and then continue downhill to the old market town of Dolgellau. We then proceed to the coastline of Cardigan Bay. We then cross the river Mawddach at its estuary over the famous Barmouth viaduct and soon we arrive at the town where time is allowed to walk around. Some of these trips offered the alternative of staying on the train, crossing the viaduct again and journeying south to Tywyn. On this trip the train passed the Friog rocks where the train clings to the rock edge.

After a few hours in Barmouth, it's time to rejoin the train for the return journey northward. This is a major holiday area and soon we are passing numerous caravans until we arrive at Harlech with its massive castle high above us on the rock face. From Harlech we approach the estuary of the river Dwyryd and cross the river into Penrhyndeudraeth and then enter Porthmadog, a busy and attractive town, once a major port and shipbuilding centre, which exported slate all over the world. From here we continue for a few miles to the attractive resort of Criccieth with its castle. Soon after passing through Criccieth we leave the Cambrian Coast Line at Afonwen and take the line that goes through some remote countryside always in view of mountains until we reach Caernarfon. The train enters Caernarfon passing its massive castle and then going through a tunnel which passes under the town square and on through Caernarfon station. We pass close to the Menai Strait with picturesque views of the island of Anglesey and the two bridges which link the island with the mainland. Soon we are passing through Bangor station and then onwards along the coast with spectaculour views of the eastern tip of Anglesey and Puffin Island and in the distance the Great Orme.

Then we pass through Conwy as the train tunnels through the ancient town walls, past the castle, over the river and soon we are back in Llandudno. This trip of about 155 miles provided in those days the only practical way of seeing such a variety of scenery and locations in one day. No coach companies offered such a trip as it would have taken too long on the roads as they were in those days and few would attempt the journey by car for the same reason.

A unique trip on a 'toastrack tram'

It is now Thursday and the week is passing by all too soon for the holiday family and after some long trips for the past three days, they now look to visit somewhere at a shorter distance. There are still some of the 'must do' things to achieve. One of these is a tram ride between Llandudno and Colwyn Bay on one of the famous 'toastracks.' Let's revive some memories and imagine we are taking this trip today. We board the toastrack at the Greenfield Road terminus in Colwyn Bay and soon it moves on to the main stop outside St. Paul's Church. Here the tram fills with passengers and the conductor starts to collect the fares, There was no central gangway on the toastracks so the conductor had to walk along a narrow ledge on one side of the tram. Such a practice would not be permitted today in our health and safety conscious society. The tram makes its way through the main street of Colwyn Bay and turns right over Brompton Avenue railway bridge continuing through a residential area of Rhos-on-sea along Whitehall Road and is soon on the promenade. From here the holiday family admires the view across the bay. In the east are the distant hills of the Vale of Clwyd which we passed on the land cruise train. Below the hills we see Rhyl bathed in sunlight and the white dome of Rhyl Pavillion (sadly demolished in the 1970s) very prominent.

Nearer to us we see the limestone quarries of Llanddulas with coasters loading the stone at the three jetties. We see also Colwyn Bay Pier. In those days, the pier was the centre of Colwyn Bay's social life for both residents and visitors. As the tram approaches the centre of Rhos-on-sea, we see another pier, somewhat longer than Colwyn Bay Pier. It originally had a landing stage for steamers but this was swept away in a storm in 1917. Until 1916 steamers called there. We now turn into Penrhyn Avenue (once called Tramway Avenue) where the track turns just a little inland through a residential area which was built during the lifetime of the tramway. We pass Colwyn Bay cricket ground but as we are on a toastrack we cannot see if there is a match in progress. To do that we would have to be on one the open top double decker trams. Next we pass the tram depot and may change crews. As it is a busy and fine summer's day, there are few trams (if any) in the depot as they are all in service. Soon we rejoin the promenade and continue on to the tramway company's private road very close to the sea. Next we turn slightly inland and pass through the residential area of Penrhyn Bay which like Rhos-on-sea developed during the life of the tramway. Next the tram climbs Penrhyn Hill on the side of the Little Orme on an elevated track parallel to the main Colwyn Bay to Llandudno road below us on the left. At the top of the hill the tram track crosses the main road and passes the old quarry village of Penrhynside. After a short distance we now enter the reserved track across Bodafon fields. This is the most interesting part of the journey and certainly makes the tram ride unique. To the right we see the blue sea of Llandudno bay between the Great and Little Ormes, and the pier in the distance and one of the steamers at the landing stage. To the left we see across the Conwy river to the mountains of Snowdonia and the Menai Strait and Anglesey in the distance.

Soon we are back in the street and continue through Craig-y-Don and then onwards towards the town centre passing the Crosville bus depot. Next we are in Mostyn Street, Llandudno's busy shopping centre and most passengers get off here, but we shall continue to the terminus. The track now turns to the left and we start on the single track section to the West Shore, where there is a fine view of the coast and mountains and in the distance Puffin Island and Anglesey. Our holiday family may well now look for something to eat and do a little shopping in Llandudno.

A tram trip up the Great Orme

Having travelled to Llandudno by tram, the holiday family will want to do another of the 'must do' things and take a trip up the Great Orme by tram. The tram station is conveniently located near the top of Mostyn Street. The tram first ascends a very steep slope passing a small residential area. This is the oldest part of the town suitably named, 'Old Street'. A glance backwards reveals a superb view of Llandudno bay. The tram continues to climb steeply passing more houses until reaching the half way station. Here all passengers get off and walk to the tram that is to ascend to the summit. If it is a clear day, the view from the top of the Great Orme is amazing. We can see the estuary of the Conwy river with the town of Conwy clearly visible and beyond we see the mountains of Snowdonia and the coast towards Bangor. Anglesey is clearly visible. In the other direction we can see the coast towards Rhyl and inland the mountains of the Clwydian Range. On a very clear day, it is possible to see the Wirral, Liverpool, Blackpool Tower, the Cumbrian mountains, and the Isle of Man. The summit of the Great Orme can indeed be said to be the roof of North Wales. There was once a semaphore telegraph station here. It was part of a chain of telegraph stations stretching from

Holyhead to Liverpool. Before the invention of wireless telegraphy, telephones, railways, motor vehicles, the fastest way to travel was on horseback, so the semaphore telegraph was the fastest way of sending a message. Shipowners in Liverpool were anxious to know the whereabouts of their ships, which had crossed the oceans. As soon as a ship was sighted off Holyhead the chain of semaphore signals began and within a few minutes the shipowners knew their ship was safely on the way home. It was assumed that any ship which had safely travelled across oceans from America or Australia would have no problem in negotiating the last few miles home to Liverpool, but this was not always the case. The rocks off the north coast of Anglesey are treacherous and the approach to the Mersey needs an experienced navigator in charge. For this reason, ships, even to this day, pick up a pilot on the north coast of Anglesey to guide them safely into Liverpool. Even so, some ships did not make it. The most famous wreck off the coast of Anglesey was the *Royal Charter* in 1859 carrying wealthy passengers bringing gold from Australia.

A trip up the Valley by diesel train

A short and popular trip for the holiday family would be to take a trip up the Conwy Valley by diesel train. Train enthusiasts and many tourists lamented the disappearance of steam trains which seemed full of life and character. Diesel multiple units on the other hand had little character and to this day I remember my thoughts when I first travelled on one. I said to myself, 'This is not a train, it's a bus on a railway line.' Despite this, British Railways' introduction of diesel multiple units on the branch line from Llandudno Junction to Blaenau Ffestiniog in 1956 was an instant success and rail fans and holiday makers alike had cause to applaud this new innovation on the line up the valley. The diesels became popular because they enabled the passengers to see a much more panoramic view of this very scenic line. The windows were bigger than the small windows of the old non corridor stock which was previously used on this line. The real bonus, specially for train enthusiasts was that is was possible to see through the glass covered driver's cab and so have a uninterrupted view of the line ahead. What makes this line so special is that it packs in such a variety of scenery in a comparatively short space. Within the one hour it takes from Llandudno to Blaenau Ffestiniog we get a varied sight of town, sea, islands, rivers and mountains, as well as dramatic waterfalls and distant moorland and the green of the valley. Let us imagine it is 1956 and we board a brand new diesel multiple unit for our afternoon trip to Blaenau Ffestiniog. We arrive early at Llandudno's impressive station as the massive clock tells us we have plenty of time. In one platform is an express for Manchester and in another is the *Welshman* for London Euston. Our diesel train pulls into another platform and we board quickly to make sure we get the front seat. There is plenty of time before the train leaves and we watch as the Stanier Class 5 pulls out with the Manchester express. About ten minutes later a tank engine heads the *Welshman* out of the station. We think, 'Why is this London express being hauled by a little tank engine and why just two coaches?' We shall find out why a bit later when we get to Llandudno Junction. Another ten minutes passes and it's time to go. We hear the 'right away' given from the station platform and the guard gives the two bell signal on the buzzer and we are off. It really does seem like a bus! As we clear the covered platforms of Llandudno station we pass a large signal box on our right which controls the lines into the station and soon after we see a smaller signal box which controls the entrance to the carriage sidings, somewhat empty today but on a summer Saturday this area is bustling with activity. We pass the ice cream factory on our left and some houses on our right and after passing under the road bridge we admire the impressive view. To the left across the golf course we see the main road and beyond it the slopes leading up to the hill where the remains of Deganwy Castle stand. To our right, across another golf course, we see the open panorama of mountain and sea. We look across to Penmaenmawr with its massive granite quarry dominating the town, and across a clear blue sea to Anglesey and Puffin Island. Soon the train reaches Deganwy and we stop at this attractive station with its open views of Conwy Castle and Telford's suspension bridge which carries the main A55 road across the river. Next, we reach Llandudno Junction and after a signal stop we slowly move into the platform of this important station. We see the tank engine which hauled the *Welshman* out of Llandudno, now on its own in a track loop. The two coaches it has hauled from Llandudno have been attached to another seven coaches and at the head of the train is a powerful Royal Scot 4-6-0 locomotive. This engine has brought the main portion of the train from Bangor, where four coaches were attached to it, two from Porthmadog and two from Pwllheli. Now we know why the London train only needed a tank engine to haul just two coaches from Llandudno to the Junction. We notice some people enjoying their lunch in the dining car.

A train pulls in on one of the down line platforms and a good number of people who have come from Prestatyn, Rhyl, Abergele and Colwyn Bay quickly cross the bridge and board our train. In the meantime the Royal Scot loco sounds its whistle and the *Welshman* departs for London. It will stop only at Colwyn Bay, Rhyl, Prestatyn, Chester and Crewe and then continue non stop to Euston. Our train is now full. It's a good thing we got on at

Llandudno and got the best seats. We notice the driver go into an office on the station and then return with the token which will give the train authority to proceed on to the single line section. Soon we are away and pass through Llandudno Junction with its factories and houses. We branch off from the main line and soon have a good view of the river which is very wide at this point. Conwy Castle is again visible and the road and railway bridges. Beyond these is an attractive wooded area know as Benarth Woods. Our train soon stops at the first station on the line, Glan Conwy which in the past was an important river port. We are soon away from the station and the line clings closely to the river bank as we move away from the main road which climbs a hill on the left. Now we are in rural surroundings with few houses or roads. We notice large flocks of birds on the river. We continue to follow the river and we notice the road is now drawing towards us again and we run between the road and river until we reach the little station of Tal-y-Cafn. Here the driver gives up the single line token and exchanges it for the token for the next section of the line. There was a river ferry here which had operated since medieval times, many travellers preferred to cross the river here rather than at Conwy where the crossing was shorter and the water calmer. A bridge was built at Tal-y-Cafn in 1897. We get on our way again and cross the hand operated level crossing. The valley now begins to get narrower as the foothills of Snowdonia draw in on our right, as we still follow the river closely. A little further on we look across the river and see a small village consisting of two long rows of houses. This is Dolgarrog where the old village was swept away when a dam high above at Llyn Eigiau burst and the village was flooded with 16 people losing their lives. From the train we can see a large factory which is an aluminium works and next to it is a power station. We notice a bridge at this point which once carried freight trains to the factory. The bridge remains open for walkers but not for vehicles. A little further along we see another village, Trefriw, which came into prominence in Edwardian days as a spa. We notice a suspension footbridge at this point which links the village of Trefriw with Llanrwst railway station which we see is named Llanrwst & Trefriw. As we approach the station we stop at the signal box where our driver exchanges the token for the next section. At the opposite platform is a freight train which when we go into the station will move forward to the signal box to collect the token we have just handed in. Llanrwst is the market town of the Conwy Valley and the shopping centre for the villages around on both sides of the river. After going through a cutting we pass Llanrwst bridge which is said to date from the 17th century. Until Conwy suspension bridge was built in 1826 this was the lowest point at which the river could be crossed.

A community has existed here from ancient times and when the bridge was built the town grew and prospered. The holiday family making this trip now really feel they are in Wales as Welsh is the predominant language being spoken by the other passengers on the train. We continue on our way up the valley and notice a great contrast between the two sides of this ever narrowing valley. On the left we see the gentle green hills of Denbighshire and on the right we see the steep slopes of Caernarfonshire. Now for the first and only time we cross the Conwy river and run through a wooded area and reach the resort of Betws-y-coed. The station is busy as people are waiting for our train and for another on the opposite platform. Most people get off our train now but others get on. This is the biggest station on the branch line with its impressive buildings, two platforms and covered footbridge. It is also the busiest station. Once more our driver takes the token to the signal box but we cannot go yet as we are waiting for another train to come off the single line section. The train arrives and gives up the token to the signalman and our driver takes the token and we are off. We now settle down in our comfortable seats for the most scenic part of the trip. The holiday family are impressed by the beauty of Betws-y-coed which they have seen before on a coach trip. Betws is the meeting point of four rivers. It is here that the rivers Llugwy, Lledr and Machno join the river Conwy. The train now leaves the Conwy and follows the river Lledr. First we go through some forest and for the next few miles we are amazed at such wonderful scenery, mountains getting close, waterfalls cascading over rocks, old bridges. We continue through this narrow valley and make a brief stop at Pont-y-Pant station. As the train sets off again, we notice the valley widens at this point into an attractive meadow with the mountains a little distance away. We are now approaching the village of Dolwyddelan which mean 'The Meadow of Gwyddelan'. Gwyddelan which means Irishman, is the name of the celtic saint who founded a community here. We stop at Dolwyddelan station and for the last time on the trip exchange tokens. This is done quickly as we there is no other train due. Dolwyddelan is steeped in history and we look up to the right and see the sturdy tower of Dolwyddelan Castle said to be the birthplace of the Llywelyn the Great, Prince of Wales. We have already passed two places with which he is associated. His stone coffin is in Llanrwst church. South of Llanrwst at Maenan there was once an Abbey which was moved there by Edward I when he built Conwy Castle. Llywelyn was a great benefactor of the Abbey in its original location at Conwy.

After passing Dolwyddelan Castle, high on our right the mountains close in and soon we stop at Roman Bridge. The small bridge there is certainly not of Roman origin. As we look to the right we see the summit of Snowdon. The scenery becomes more and more remote and it appears we are heading right into the mountains when suddenly we are plunged into a tunnel. Now we appreciate the advantage of having chosen a front seat. After less than a minute we see what looks like a pinhole of light in the distance which is the end of the tunnel. Apart from the short curve we have just negotiated, the tunnel is perfectly straight. We are now in the longest single line tunnel in Britain at 2 miles 206 yards long. We watch with eager anticipation as the pinhole gets bigger and after a little over 4 minutes we emerge from the tunnel into an amazing landscape. The holiday family seeing this for the first time feel they are in another world. There is slate everywhere. We pass either side of the state tips and soon arrive at Blaenau Ffestiniog North station. Now the tourists know without doubt they are in Wales. Apart from other tourists, there is not a word of English heard as the tourists listen fascinated as the people of this slate quarry community speak to each other only in Welsh. There is a little time to explore the town and to admire the mountains and the distant view of the Vale of Ffestiniog down to Porthmadog. All too soon it is time to return to Llandudno. The train we board for the return journey is a through train to Rhyl so Llandudno passengers will need to change at Llandudno Junction. We return to the coast after a wonderful afternoon and agree that this trip has been special.

A visit to Conwy

Another short trip that the holiday family might take would be to Conwy, just a 20 minute bus trip from Colwyn Bay or Llandudno or 30 minutes by train from Rhyl. The holiday maker immediately becomes aware that Conwy has a different atmosphere from that of Llandudno, Colwyn Bay and Rhyl. The approach to the town over Telford's suspension bridge (as it was until 1958), with the castle towering above is impressive. Conwy Castle was one described by a historian as a building that looked more like it was designed by an artist rather than a military architect. The tourist would find plenty to do in this little town. A visit to the castle would be another 'must do thing'. Conwy is steeped in history and was an established town when Llandudno was no more than a hamlet on the side of the Great Orme, Rhyl was a few houses by the sea and Colwyn Bay was not even thought of. Conwy is unique in Wales, having in addition to the castle, the complete circuit of thirteenth century town walls. (In England only the cities of Chester and York can boast this). A visit to Conwy would not be complete without a visit to the old sixteenth century town house, Plas Mawr and the even older Aberconwy House. Conwy Parish Church is also well worth a visit, the foundation of which (as Aberconwy Abbey) pre dates the castle. The holiday family will be sure to visit Conwy Quay and go into the smallest house in Britain and watch the many fishing boats landing their catch, and maybe buy some fresh fish to take back to their guest house and ask their hosts to cook it. If time permits the holiday makers may take a boat trip up the river Conwy to Trefriw where in Edwardian days paddle steamers took people to Trefriw to sample the iron and sulphur waters of the spa.

A trip on the 'Welsh Dragon'

People who came on holiday to the main resorts of Llandudno, Colwyn Bay and Rhyl would want to explore all three towns regardless of which one they stayed in. The transport undertakings of the day all provided the means to do this. There were frequent bus services linking Llandudno, Rhos-on-sea,

Colwyn Bay, Abergele, Towyn and Rhyl and also a tram service between Colwyn Bay and Llandudno. British Railways (as it was then called), ran an 'express' train between Llandudno and Rhyl and named it *The Welsh Dragon*. Although not an express in the same style as the *Irish Mail,* the *Welshman* or *The Emerald Isle Express*, it nevertheless provided a faster town to town link than did the bus services.

Let us imagine we are in Rhyl in the 1950s and about to take a trip on the *Welsh Dragon* to Llandudno. We make our way to Rhyl Railway Station outside of which is a bus station for buses travelling in the direction of Abergele. In winter these services terminated at the main bus station in High Street with the other services, but in summer when there were many extra buses on these routes, it was necessary for the Abergele direction services to depart from outside the railway station. This also provided a useful connection to and from the trains for people staying at the many caravan sites between Rhyl and Abergele. On entering the station, we first go to the large ticket hall and buy our tickets for Llandudno. We make our way to the platforms and notice a large crowd waiting for the London train while to our left people make their way to the bay platform for the stopping train to Chester. As we are bound for Llandudno we make our way over the bridge to the platforms on the other side of the station where there are three trains in. The train on the through platform is an express for Holyhead and there is a train in each of the two bay platforms. One is for Denbigh and the other is our train, the *Welsh Dragon* for Llandudno. It is just a three coach train of non corridor stock hauled by a tank engine. Soon we are on our way. On our right we see the large signal box controlling the complicated junction at this end the station and next we pass the Rhyl engine sheds where a number of old engines are in steam. These are used on the Vale of Clwyd line. As the train gathers speed we pass the famous Marine Lake on our right and see the fun fair in the distance and the steam hauled miniature railway which goes around the lake. Soon we are crossing Foryd Bridge and a glance to our left reveals a fine view of the Vale of Clwyd and the hills on each side. It is a sunny day so we catch a glimpse of the tall spire of the Marble Church at Bodelwyddan and the square tower of St. Asaph Cathedral in the distance. Just after the end of the bridge, we see a junction on the left which is where the Denbigh line joins the main line, controlled by Foryd Signal Box. We now enter Kinmel Bay and notice many recently built bungalows largely occupied by retired people. Soon we pass under the road bridge and on both sides of the track are large numbers of caravans, standing close together where many people take advantage of good value holiday accommodation. The train now starts to slow down and to our left we see the market town of Abergele and soon we pull into Pensarn station, the station being officially designated Abergele & Pensarn, the town of Abergele being about three quarters of a mile inland. We notice the camping coaches on our right as some people from them get on the train. As we leave Pensarn station we see on our left a wooded area in which is set Gwrych Castle. This is not a castle in the military sense but was built as a family mansion, but now sold and used as a tourist centre. There is now an open view of the sea on the right and in the distance we see one of the steamers on route from Llandudno to Liverpool. A little further on we see a small tower high on the hills to our left. This is to commemorate those who lost their lives in a train accident at this spot. A pick up goods train had stopped at Llysfaen between Abergele and Colwyn Bay to shunt some wagons into a siding. As the siding was too short the train had to be divided and some shunting operations took place on the main line. The *Irish*

91

Mail on its way to Holyhead was due to pass in a matter of 15 minutes, but as the Mail approached some of the wagons broke away and started to run down a falling gradient. Some of these wagons were carrying paraffin and others timber so when the *Irish Mail* collided with them the engine became covered with paraffin, the consequence being a major fire. The leading coaches of the *Irish Mail* were burnt out and 32 people lost their lives. The driver was unharmed as he jumped out seconds before the crash. The coaches at the rear were not damaged. So as we pass this scene we feel a sense of relief at the safety regulations that apply to our train. As we pass Llanddulas signal box the quadruple track becomes double and at this point trains are often waiting to enter the double track section on busy summer Saturdays. A little further we look to the right and see a coaster loading limestone at one of the Llanddulas quarry jetties. Soon the train plunges into Penmaenrhos tunnel. This headland at one time went into the sea until quarrying operations reduced much of its grandeur. If there are blasting operations at the quarry our train will be halted at Llysfaen signal box until the blasting is completed, as a safety precaution. On emerging from the tunnel a grand vista of Colwyn Bay opens to us. We see the curved three mile long bay with Rhos-on-sea at the far end and beyond it the Little Orme and in the far distance we just catch a glimpse of the summit of the Great Orme. Before long we are running on a high embankment parallel to Colwyn Bay promenade where crowds of people are enjoying the sunny weather on the sandy beach. As we approach the Groes Viaduct over the entrance to Eirias Park, we see a number of chalets below the railway embankment. These are not for residential occupation but can be hired for a day or a week during the daytime, being very popular with local families. The train now slows down to stop at Colwyn Bay station. As we approach the station we see Colwyn Bay Pier on our right, a major social centre for residents and visitors alike. We may even see the town band entertaining a crowd of people on the pier. Although not as big as Rhyl station, Colwyn Bay station is nonetheless impressive and has four through platforms. The promenade is hidden from view by a large glass screen to protect waiting passengers from northerly winds. On leaving the station the line moves inland a little and passes Bryn Euryn to the right, a hill which dominates the town of Colwyn Bay. We think that if time permits before the end of the holiday, it may be worth climbing to the summit to experience the 360 degree view. Next we pass the village of Mochdre whose railway station has long closed but the signal box is retained for use at busy times. It was at Mochdre that the first water troughs in the world were installed to enable Holyhead bound expresses to proceed without having to stop to take on water. The scenery changes somewhat here as we get a grand view of the mountains of Snowdonia beyond the Conwy Valley. We are now approaching Llandudno Junction, very much the cross roads of North Wales. As we approach the station the Conwy Valley branch line comes in from our left. The station has eight platforms, four for through trains and four bay platforms. After a short stop, the *Welsh Dragon* leaves the main line to our left and takes the branch line to Llandudno, crossing the main A55 road where a long queue of traffic has built up. The remaining three miles of our journey on this short branch line are full of interest. Conwy Castle and bridge are clearly seen across the river with an assortment of small boats. and beyond the steep sides of Conwy Mountain. Soon the train stops at Deganwy's scenic station on the bank of the river and then we are on our way to Llandudno. To our left is an amazing vista of coast and mountains, and in the distance the Island of Anglesey and Puffin Island. Now the train slows down on the approach to Llandudno. We pass through two golf courses, one on each side and then after passing under the bridge we pass the carriage sidings and enter the very impressive Llandudno station. The station with its five platforms and overall glass roof has all the atmosphere of a big terminal station, as taxis come and go on the central road between two of the platforms. We leave the train and notice the large station clock, so typical of a major station. In a journey of just 18 miles we have experienced an amazing variety of scenery and places of interest.

Back to Rhyl by bus

Now as we remain in the 1950s in our imagination, let's return from Llandudno to Rhyl by bus. In order to take the full journey we board bus number 409 at the West Shore terminus. There are a number of buses and also a tram waiting at this terminus. Before we board the bus we take a look at the view across to Anglesey and the western slopes of the Great Orme. If we are lucky we may see some of the wild goats that live on the Orme. Now it's time to get on the bus, a comfortable Bristol Lodekka. Not many passengers board here so we go upstairs and take the front seats which will give us a good view throughout the journey. The journey begins along Gloddaeth Avenue, a perfectly straight road which passes through a residential area before arriving at the Hooson's Corner stop where many people board the bus. This is a busy place and there are three buses at the stop and two trams in the middle of the road. Much to the consternation of the tram driver our bus gets away from the stop first which means it will pick up most of the passengers at the very busy stop outside *Marks & Spencers* in Mostyn Street. After this stop the bus is full. Mostyn Street is packed with shoppers, locals and tourists alike.

After a stop at the North Western Hotel a few passengers get on but they have to stand, but others are left behind. We then proceed along Mostyn Broadway and stop at the Crosville Depot to change crews. During this time the tram overtakes the bus and will get to the stop at Queens Road, Craig-y-Don first. The new driver quickly gets the bus away and as the tram is taking on passengers at Craig-y-Don, the bus now overtakes the tram. Here, our bus turns left into Carmen Silva Road and on to the promenade while the tram behind us continues along Mostyn Broadway and into Bodafon fields. As we travel by bus along the promenade we get a good view of Llandudno Bay with the Great and Little Ormes. To our right we see the fields and the tram making good headway. Who will get to the top of Bryn y Bia Road first, the bus or the tram? We have to make two more stops so when we get to the top of Bryn y Bia Road, the tram has beaten us. We now descend Penrhyn Hill on the side of the Little Orme and run parallel to the tram which is on its reserved track. At the bottom of Penrhyn Hill, we take the main road through Penrhyn Bay and the tram takes the road to the left towards the promenade. We now pass through Penrhyn Bay, a residential area popular with retired people. A few people get off the bus here and as we continue, we pass the golf course on our left and in the distance see the tram on its company's private road along the sea front. To our right we see in the distance the village of Mochdre. At this point we cross a tiny stream almost too small to notice. This stream known as the Afon Ganol *'central river'* marks the boundary between Caernarfonshire and Denbighshire as at the same time we pass from the Urban District of Llandudno to the Borough of Colwyn Bay. In the distant past the river Conwy entered the sea here, having flowed through Mochdre. At the point where the Afon Ganol enters the sea, it is said that the

Welsh Prince Madog sailed and discovered the American continent long before the time of Columbus. Now our bus climbs a short hill and ahead of us we see Bryn Euryn. We may want to get off the bus here to take the steep climb to the top. On our way up we would pass the ruins of Llys Euryn, the old palace of Edynfed Fychan who was seneschal to the Prince of Wales, Llywelyn the Great in the late twelfth and early thirteenth centuries. But we continue on our bus journey and on our left we pass the ancient church of Llandrillo which was the place of worship of Ednyfed Fychan. The bus continues to a cross roads where we turn left at the traffic lights into Rhos Road, where a tramway once ran to the sea from a quarry on Bryn Euryn. Soon we find ourselves in Rhos-on-sea as the bus turns on to the promenade. Many people get off here and also a good number get on. We have time here to admire the view of the bay and immediately opposite about ten miles away is Rhyl. We can see the sun shining on the pavillion and the backdrop of the Clwydian range of mountains. We can see all along the coast from Rhyl at this point. We set off from Rhos-on-sea where we rejoin the tram route and continue through a residential area and cross the railway bridge under which the main Chester to Holyhead line passes and we are in the part of Colwyn Bay known as the West End. We continue through a residential area and get to the stop at the top of Station Road in the centre of Colwyn Bay. Many people get off here which is just as well as there is a long queue waiting to board the bus. After a short wait while passengers get on and off the bus, we are again on our way through the busy town centre of Colwyn Bay. At the top of the hill, we see a tram at the Greenfield Road terminus waiting to return to Llandudno. We climb another steep hill and get to the main gates of Eirias Park. These gates were given to the park in commemoration of the National Eisteddfod of Wales held at the park in 1947. Many people get off here to enjoy all the amenities that the park offers. We follow the southern boundary of the park and in the distance there is a view of the sea. Next the bus goes down a hill into the village of Old Colwyn, originally Colwyn. Many people get off the bus here but not so many get on. We cross the bridge in the centre of the village and to our right we see the houses of the old village. We have already noticed on our bus trip that Colwyn Bay is very hilly, unlike Llandudno which is basically on flat land. We now ascend another steep hill to Penmaenrhos, locally known as Penmaen Head. From here there is a spectaculour view of the whole of Colwyn Bay and the Little Orme in the distance. Most buses from Llandudno terminate here but we continue our journey towards the village of Llanddulas with its limestone quarries, the base of the quarry being visible at some depth from the top deck of the bus. We stop at Llanddulas village and continue on our way towards Aberegle, first passing through a green area. We are now running parallel to the railway and see the same sights we saw on our train journey. We pass the entrance to Gwyrch Castle where many people board the bus to return to Rhyl after a trip to the castle. Soon we are in the town centre of Abergele. Abergele is an old market town which was an established community long before tourism developed. In fact until the middle of the nineteenth century there was no community of note between Abergele and Conwy. If it is the monthly fair day we shall see the stalls on the street selling their wares. There is also a weekly agricultural market in the town. We now turn left into Water Street and continue down the hill for about three quarters of a mile through a residential area to the suburb of Pensarn and stop outside the railway station. The next five miles to Rhyl are very much a holiday coast as we pass through

Towyn and then Kinmel Bay with their caravans. Many people board the bus at these stops, both tourists from the caravan camps and local people from the growing housing development. We cross the river Clwyd and enter Rhyl, seeing the railway bridge on our right. We turn off the promenade into Wellington Road and soon we are at the bus station outside the railway station after a journey of an hour and a quarter from Llandudno.

Last Day of the Holiday

It is Friday already and tomorrow the holiday family will be heading back home, so how will they spend their last day in North Wales? Friday was always a quiet day as regards train and coach trips. Maybe the money had run out! Friday would usually be spent exploring the town where they were staying and doing some last minute shopping and buying some gifts to take to the folks at home. So what did the three main resorts offer in those days?

Each town was (and still is) different. There was no shortage of shops in Llandudno, both the multiple chain stores and family owned shops. Also there was plenty to do in exploring the town and immediate area. A walk (or bus ride) on the Marine Drive around Great Orme would be an interesting way to spend a few hours, or a visit to the Happy Valley with its open air theatre or a walk through Haulfre Gardens. For the more energetic, a trip to the open air swimming pool at Deganwy would be a pleasant few hours. At the other end of the town, a good way to spend some time would be to explore the Little Orme or take a walk through Gloddaeth Woods.

Colwyn Bay offered much for the tourists to do. As far as shopping was concerned Colwyn Bay specialised in high qualtity family owned stores whose wares ranged from quality furniture, pottery and china, to clothes. Colwyn Bay's Eirias Park provided a wonderful day out for visitors and residents alike. It had a miniature golf course, tennis courts, a boating lake, a pool for model yachts, a bowling green, a midget golf course, a puppet theatre, swings and roundabouts, a cafe, rock gardens, a football ground, and sports arena. There was always something to do and those of us who grew up in Colwyn Bay need never say we were bored. The town had six cinemas, including one in Old Colwyn and one in Rhos-on-sea and a repertory theatre in the town itself. There were smaller parks at Old Colwyn, Rhos-on-sea and Mochdre. Colwyn Bay's Victoria Pier was an important social centre for tourists and residents alike. It possessed a fine theatre which regularly featured entertainment. The pier had a cafe and a bar. There was a band stand on the pier where the Colwyn Town Band played to entertain visitors who relaxed in the sun on their deck chairs. The band also played at Old Colwyn and Rhos-on-sea. An open air swimming pool at Rhos-on-sea proved popular.

For those who wished to explore the promenade area Colwyn Bay Corporation provided a minibus service, known locally as the 'runabouts' between the end of the promenade in Old Colwyn to Rhos-on-sea. In later years the service was temporarily extended to the top of Wynnstay Road in Old Colwyn. An additional bus ran from Rhos-on-sea and Colwyn Bay up the hill from the promenade to the centre of Eirias Park.

The holiday family at Rhyl had plenty to do. There was a large variety of shops offering plenty of choice of something to buy to take home. Rhyl's two fun fairs provided a good time for all the family. A trip on the miniature train around the Marine Lake was a 'must do thing' for visitors to Rhyl. There were plenty of cinemas and theatres including the famous Pavilion theatre with its distinctive white dome which reflected the sunlight in this resort known as 'Sunny Rhyl'. An interesting way of spending a few hours would be a walk through the botanical gardens at the east end of the town or a walk on the pier.

All three resorts had the usual seaside town facilities without which a seaside holiday would be incomplete, Punch and Judy, donkey rides, sea bathing, building sandcastles for the young, and for the older visitors simply to hire a deck chair and sit on the beach or the promenade and enjoy the sunshine.

Back home

Saturday has come all too soon and the holiday family are preparing to go back home, carrying suitcases which seem to be twice as heavy as when they came! Before they leave many will book for the same week next year at the same place as they decided they have not seen half there is to see in North Wales. Those staying in private houses say their 'good byes' and 'thank yous' to their hosts and promise to keep in touch when new friendships had been formed. So the holiday family make their way to railway station or coach station or maybe to Llandudno Pier to return home by sea, and soon they are on their way home.

What about a second week?

Most people had one week's holiday to the North Wales coast but the lucky ones had two weeks. Many of these had been before and soon realised that a week is not really long enough to see all that North Wales has to offer the tourist. So having done all the 'must do things' what else was there in those post war years for the holiday family to do for a second week? There was plenty to do so let's see what the holiday family does on their second week. Saturday would be spent planning what they would do for the week and taking a second look at the handbills advertising the various excursions.

A short trip into the countryside

Sunday would be a quiet day as the transport systems did not really get going until lunch time. Some short coach trips into the countryside would be available.

The Island of Anglesey

On Monday of the second week the holiday family will begin to look for a full day trip, so they would take advantage of one of the many day trips offered to the Island of Anglesey. There were three ways of doing this, one being a coach trip from Llandudno, Colwyn Bay or Rhyl, another would be to travel by sea from Llandudno to Menai Bridge and then take a coach tour of the island. Another way would be to travel to Bangor by train and then a coach trip around the island. Anglesey is a big island, in fact it is the largest British offshore island south of the Hebrides, so it takes the full day to explore the island. The coaches would usually start by travelling alongside the Menai Strait from Menai Bridge to Beaumaris. There would be a stop at Beaumaris for coffee and some time would be allowed in this interesting little town where there would be much to see for the tourist, the castle being the most popular. Beaumaris is the historic county town of Anglesey and was at one time linked with Liverpool by paddle steamers. It is a pleasant place simply to sit and look across the Menai Strait towards Bangor and the mountains of Snowdonia in the distance and further away the Great Orme and Llandudno looking like a plate between the Great Orme and Little Orme. On leaving Beaumaris the tour would take the holiday makers along the east coast of Anglesey passing Red Wharf Bay and the comparatively modern seaside resort of of Benllech. After leaving Benllech, the next village is Moelfre, a small fishing village. Moelfre lifeboat station is famous for being one of the busiest and for having been involved in some very heroic rescues. The tour continues on the north coast of the island passing Amlwch, once the centre for copper mining and in its busiest days was the second largest town in Wales. Next we come to Cemaes and after turning on to the west coast arrive at the port town of Holyhead on the separate Holy Island, linked to the main island by a causeway. Holyhead has for centuries been the main port linking Wales and Ireland, this being the reason for building the North Wales coast railway and the main A5 road. There would be a stop for lunch either at Holyhead or at nearby Trearddur. All the tours would give an opportunity to visit the famous South Stack lighthouse by crossing the high suspension footbridge. Following this, there would be the return journey on the main A5 road.

A different direction

It is now Tuesday of the second week so is there anymore for our holiday family to see? There certainly is! Most of the trips the holiday family have made so far have been towards Snowdonia or the west coast, so on Tuesday of the second week, they may well take a trip in the opposite direction. The coach trip begins in Llandudno or Colwyn Bay and first gets to the old market town of Abergele. Abergele was an established town long before the resorts of Llandudno, Colwyn Bay and Rhyl were. From Abergele the coach continues to a popular stopping place, the Marble Church at Bodelwyddan. Next the coach continues to St. Asaph where time may be allowed to visit the Cathedral. From here we retrace our steps up the agricultural Vale of Clwyd to the market town of Denbigh with its castle at the top of the hill. From Denbigh the coach takes its passengers over the wild moorland of Mynydd Hiraethog (Denbigh Moors) where sheep graze on the lonely moorland. The old shooting lodge of Gwylfa Hiraethog can be seen on the right. In the distance on a clear day the mountains of Snowdonia can be seen to the west and the estuary of the river Dee to the east. As we drop down from the moors we reach the main A5 road at the village of Pentrefoelas. If it is a half day trip the coach will turn right here and continue to Betws-y-coed where a stop will be made for a cup of tea and then back to the coast via the Conwy Valley. The coach may well take the tourists down the west side of the Conwy Valley giving time to visit Gwydir Castle and Trefriw Woolen Mills. However, if the trip is for the whole day, the coach will turn left at Pentrefoelas and proceed through Corwen to Llangollen. This is a small. attractive town on the banks of the river Dee. In the post war years Llangollen became famous as the town where Wales welcomes the world. There was an idea that Wales with her tradition of hospitality would be the ideal country to do something to bring the nations of Europe together in an atmosphere of peace. Wales has for centuries held a national cultural festival, the National Eisteddfod, so this tradition was now widened to hold an International Eisteddfod also. This was done by holding a festival of music and dancing and inviting people from all countries to take part in competition. It was an instant success and has been repeated every year since. So every year in the first week of July this little town is host to the world where people are seen in national costume and the music and dancing traditions of every country are heard. If the holiday family were in Wales on the first week in July, this trip would be really special. After spending some time in Llangollen the next destination would be the impressive Horseshoe Pass, so named because the road clings to the mountainside in the shape of a horseshoe as it goes around the pass. From here the tourists may head for Wrexham to do some shopping and then back to the coast, or take the shorter way back after a stop in the old market town of Ruthin.

Llŷn Peninsula

On Wednesday of the second week, the holiday family may make a coach trip a little further afield to the far tip of northwest Wales. This coach trip would begin with a trip along the coast to Bangor, where a short stop would be made. A visit would be made to Bangor cathedral, the oldest cathedral in Britain in continuous use. Bangor is also famous for its university and is very much the educational and ecclesiastical centre of this part of Wales.

The holiday family now re-join the coach for the short trip alongside the Menai Strait to Caernarfon. On arrival here, the visitor immediately notices the castle and if time allows visits it. Lunch will probably be taken in Caernarfon before heading south through remote mountain country to Pwllheli, the market town for the Llŷn peninsula. This is a historic pilgrim route. If it is market day, the tourists will find plenty to interest them, otherwise they may go to the harbour and promenade. Some coach trips would take their passengers further afield to Nefyn on the north coast of the peninsula and then on past Porthoer *(Whistling Sands)* to Aberdaron, the village at the 'land's end' of North Wales. If time was allowed at Aberdaron some of the tourists may take a walk up to the hamlet of Uwchmynydd and on to Mynydd Mawr where a view could be obtained of Ynys Enlli (Bardsey Island), the destination of the old pilgrim routes, where it is said 20,000 saints are buried.

Then it is back to Aberdaron to join the coach and travel back to Pwllheli, this time on the south coast of the peninsula. As it is Wednesday, the coach driver may stop to give us time to look round Pwllheli's large street market and buy some of the famous 'Number 8 Rock.' Soon after Pwllheli the coach passes the famous Butlin's Holiday Camp which at the height of season accommodated as many as 10,000 guests.

Some day coach trips were available here. We continue through the village of Llanystumdwy, childhood home of the World War 1 Prime Minister, David Lloyd George who was MP for Caernarfon. Next we reach the little resort of Criccieth where no stop would be complete without sampling some of the famous Cadwaladars ice cream. From Criccieth it is but a short journey to Porthmadog. The 1950s tourists would see a new attraction at Porthmadog. These were the very early days of the start of railway preservation. The Talyllyn Railway at Tywyn further south had been taken over by enthusiasts. In fact it never closed as the enthusiasts group took over when British Railways, Western Region closed it. At Porthmadog, however, the Ffestiniog Railway built to carry slate from the quarries to the harbour at Porthmadog had closed. It was reopened in stages by enthusiasts. If time allowed, the hoilday family would take a short trip on this railway - more about this in a later chapter. Near to Porthmadog, the coach may call at the Italianate village of Portmeirion, designed by local architect Clough Williams Ellis. Some trips would go north from Porthmadog through the impressive Aberglaslyn Pass to the mountain village of Beddgelert. The name means 'The grave of Gelert.' There is a popular legend as to how the village got its name. Prince Llywelyn the Great had a palace here and the story goes that one day he went out hunting and left his faithful dog, Gelert to look after his baby son. When Llywelyn returned, the room where he left the baby was in a shambles. The cot was overturned and his dog Gelert was covered in blood. Llywelyn's first thought was that the dog had killed the baby and in a fit of anger, he drew his sword and killed the dog. Then he heard the baby crying and saw near the baby a dead wolf. The dog had killed the wolf and saved the baby. The legend says that Llywelyn was filled with remorse and never was the same man again. It is said he named the place Bedd Gelert in honour of his dog which he buried there. It is unlikely that the story is true. It is true that Llywelyn had a palace here, but the local belief is that the story was made up by a publican to get people to stay in his hotel and allocated an area where the grave was said to be. There are in fact similar stories in other villages in Europe. Whether the story is true or not, tourists still go to Beddgelert to this day to look at Gelert's grave. From here the coach continues north through the pass of Nant Gwynant, said by many to be the most beautiful mountain pass in Snowdonia, the views from Llyn (Lake) Glaslyn being outstanding. From here we ascend a steep hill to arrive at Penygwryd and we are joined from the left by the road from Llanberis which the holiday family travelled on the previous week from the Snowdon trip. The tourists of the 50s and 60s would be interested to be told that the inn at Penygwryd was the base for the training camp for the climbers who were the first to make a successful climb to the summit of Everest in 1953. It was here, in the mountains of Snowdonia that they prepared themselves for that massive expedition. From here the coach takes the holiday makers to Capel Curig, Betws-y-coed and back to the north coast down the Conwy Valley.

A marathon day trip

By now it is Thursday of the second week and there is yet more to see, so how about a trip to Aberystwyth? This is a long trip and took a coach of the day at least three hours to make the trip, but with some spectaculour scenery on the way. The coach would leave Llandudno early just after 9am as soon as the hotels had finished serving breakfast. The journey takes the route up the Conwy Valley passing through Llanrwst and Betws-y-coed before climbing the steep Lledr Valley through the attractive village of

Dolwyddelan and then over the Crimea Pass (named after prisoners of war from the Crimean War who built it), and then into the slate town of Blaenau Ffestiniog. Slates from the quarries here were exported all over the world. It was at one time one of the largest towns in Wales. From Blaenau the coach continues through the old village of Llan Ffestiniog with fine views down the Vale of Ffestiniog to the coast at Porthmadog. Next, the route climbs a steep road and passes through the village of Trawsfynydd with its nuclear power station (now closed). When this was built it caused some controversy but local opinion was mixed especially as it provided employment in an area where the slate industry was in decline. Soon we reach the attractive little market town of Dolgellau, the county town of Meirionydd, where a stop is made for coffee. Tourists who have been on the North Wales Land Cruise will have passed through Dolgellau before en route from Corwen to Barmouth. Dolgellau is dominated by the mountain Cader Idris, the principal mountain in south Snowdonia. A local legend says that whoever climbs Cader Idris and remains there all night will either become a poet or will go mad. Our route out of Dolgellau climbs steeply around the base of Cader Idris and then through the pass known as Tal-y-Llyn where the road clings to the mountain edge and below is a dramatic view of Tal-y-llyn lake and beyond the valley to the seaside resort of Tywyn.

Next we pass through the quarrying village of Corris and then cross the bridge over the river Dyfi into the town of Machynlleth in Montgomeryshire. This town has an important place in Welsh history. It was for a time the capital of Wales when Owain Glyndwr set up his parliament here. We continue on the south bank of the river Dyfi looking across to the coast of Meirionydd and the little resort of Aberdyfi. At this point the Dyfi forms the boundary between North and South Wales as we are now in the county of Ceredigion. In the distance is the seaside resort of Borth as we now pass through farming county and continue for a few more miles when we cross the brow of a hill and the town of Aberystwyth suddenly appears below us. We proceed down the hill and are soon in the centre of the town. Aberystwyth has developed into a modern university town and seaside resort. The development begin in the mid nineteenth century and the town was well established as a seaside resort by the time the University was built in 1872. Tourists from the North Wales coast who are visiting Aber (as it is called by the locals) will find some similarities with Llandudno such as the row of hotels along the promenade, a great rock called Constitution Hill with a funicular railway to the top, and a pier. It is smaller than Llandudno and the pier is but a fraction of the length of Llandudno Pier. The day trippers from the North Wales coast will find plenty of places to choose from to have lunch in Aberystwyth and will have a few hours during the afternoon to explore the town. The return journey was too long to get back to Llandudno for the evening meal at the hotels so the coach would usually stop en route. Sometimes the coach would take a slightly different route on the return journey and stop for something to eat in Bala.

It's Friday and the second week of the holiday is nearly over and holiday family probably wake up feeling a little tired after their marathon trip to Aberystwyth the day before. So Friday would be a leisurely day, doing some shopping or perhaps making one more visit to a favourite place. Sometimes as well as buying gifts to take home to friends and family, the holiday makers who stayed in small Bed & Breakfast establishments would often buy gifts for their hosts, specially if they return to the same place year after year.

Saturday would be the day to travel home. Few, if any visitors would stay for a third week as in those days most people only had two weeks holiday from work and a three week holiday would be beyond the budget of most people.

Some other trips

There were two other popular trips that British Railways (as it was in those days) ran from the North Wales coast. I have not included these in the tourist itinerary in this chapter for two reasons. They were provided as much for local people as for tourists and they were trips outside Wales. One was a rail/sea trip to Dublin and the other was a trip along the coast to Chester.

The Dublin trip is worthy of mention here as the Chester to Holyhead railway was originally built for communication between London and Dublin. In the 1950s there was one crossing each night between Holyhead and Dun Laoghaire and in the summer additional daytime crossings. The *Irish Mail* from London did not stop between Chester and Holyhead, but there was a train from Manchester to Holyhead which stopped at Prestatyn, Rhyl, Colwyn Bay, Llandudno Junction and Bangor which arrived in Holyhead at around 2am, making a convenient connection for the 3.25am crossing to Dun Laoghaire. This train ran all the year round so provided a convenient connection from the North Wales coast stations. Passengers then travelled from Dun Laoghaire to Dublin by train where they arrived at about 8am. which gave a whole day in Dublin before returning on the ferry at 8.45pm from Dun Laoghaire. There was a connecting train from Holyhead to Manchester which stopped at Bangor, Colwyn Bay and Rhyl where it arrived about 2.15am. But this train ran only in summer so in the winter anyone wishing to get to the coastal stations would have to remain on the ship at Holyhead until the following morning and catch the 7.30am. *Emerald Isle Express* to London which stopped at the principal stations along the coast. In the summer there were also shorter day trips from Holyhead to Dublin with connecting trains.

Another destination that the railways advertised was a day trip to Chester. Although North Wales people generally preferred Liverpool for major shopping, Chester was nevertheless popular with locals and tourists.

Chapter 8

LIVING IN A SEASIDE RESORT

People who live in seaside resorts, particularly if they have been born and brought up in a one, as I was, would be asked two questions by visitors. The first was, 'Where do you go for your holidays?' and the second, 'What is it like in a seaside resort in winter?'

Most people who lived in seaside resorts in the 1950s (and to a lesser extent in the 1960s) did not often go on holiday. Everything was there for us. School holidays were never boring. There was always something to do. We would spend hours on the railway embankment with our notebooks and pencils and the Ian Allan locomotive abc s. The highlight of the day for us was the passage of the *Irish Mail*. Somehow we just hoped to get a rare engine hauling this principal express, but that rarely if ever happened. It was always hauled by one the Britannia Pacifics of Holyhead shed 70045/49. So rather than go home for lunch, our mothers would give us a large box of sandwiches to keep us going so we could see this express passing at lunchtime. Sometimes we would go to Eirias Park and play golf or hire a rowing boat or paddle boat on the lake, all in sight of the railway. On a warm day we would go to the swimming pool at Rhos-on-sea. Indeed all the facilities available to visitors were available to locals too. The weekly railway runabout ticket was a good value way of having a different day trip every day. A 'must do' with this ticket was taking a train to Chester in the morning, then travelling non stop from Chester to Holyhead on the *Irish Mail* and returning from Holyhead to Colwyn Bay on a late afternoon train. The steamers from Llandudno also provided a weekly ticket and this enabled us to occupy another week of the holidays. If it rained there were six cinemas to choose from. During the two weeks my parents were on holiday we would usually go on trips in the car each day - yes, we were one of the lucky families who had a car because my father was a mechanic and he knew how to repair them. There was always somewhere interesting to go within a day's journey of home. In later years we did have some family holidays further afield. I remember one year we went to South Wales and the south of England. Another year we toured Scotland going up the west coast to the far north and returning down the east coast. This was a marathon holiday and with my interest in all forms of public transport, I was fascinated by the ferries linking the Clyde resorts and the Western Isles, and the short ferries of which there were many in Scotland in those days. We never went on holiday abroad. From my youngest days, I can remember two day trips that were made every year which became somewhat of a ritual. In the summer there would be a day trip to Chester Zoo. This seemed so far away that it was like going to another planet. The other would be a train trip to Liverpool for shopping usually sometime in late November/early December. In those days the North Wales towns did not have the very big stores that Liverpool did. This was for me and for most of my contemporaries my first visit to a major city. I remember being fascinated with the escalators (or moving stairs as I called them). It would not be at all unusual to hear Welsh spoken in Liverpool, as so many Welsh families went there for major shopping expeditions and there were many Welsh speaking people living in Liverpool. In fact many of the major stores were founded by Welsh families. The link between Liverpool and North Wales goes back to the early days of steamships when the sea route was the principal way of travelling from Liverpool to North Wales. It is not surprising that Liverpool was in those days referred to as the capital of North

Wales! On one of such trips I can remember we got off the train at Old Colwyn station, on what I think was probably the last train ever to stop there.

In the 1950s and 60s in the holiday resorts most people worked in tourist related employment so summer holidays were not possible. Those who had holidays would take them in October or even later into the winter. There was a designated day in October, usually the first Monday which was known as 'Tradesmen's Holiday' when all the shops in the coastal resorts would close and the shopkeepers would go to Liverpool for the day. There would be extra trains and coaches that day and the coastal resorts themselves were deserted. It was a kind of local bank holiday. This tradition had disappeared by the late 1960s. A similar tradition existed in the inland towns and villages and in the more Welsh speaking areas. This was known as *'Dydd Llun Pawb'*. It was usually on the third Monday in October and was linked with harvest festival services in the churches and chapels and the school half term week. All the shops closed on that day. This tradition continued well into the 1980s and some churches and chapels still have their harvest festivals on that day, but it is generally no longer a public holiday.

From the mid 1960s onwards people who lived in seaside resorts started to go on package holidays abroad like everyone else. Local people who worked in the tourist industry and particularly those who owned hotels and guest houses would of course have to take their holidays in winter. This would mean going abroad to a warmer climate and usually leaving a minimal staff to supervise the work of maintenance, decorating and refurbishment while the hotel remained closed to paying guests. People who did not depend on the tourist trade for their living took their holidays in the summer.

Seaside Towns in Winter

The seaside resorts were quieter in winter but certainly not dead. The tourist facilities closed for the winter, but there remained much to do and the cinemas were open all the year round. Many local people enjoyed the winter for the very reason that the towns were not so busy. Various clubs and societies flourished in winter and even before the age of television, people in seaside towns were never short of something to do.

Local Employment

At this point it is relevant to mention how employment trends in the area changed over the years. As the seaside towns began to grow rapidly from the mid nineteenth century onwards, they developed with two purposes. Firstly as holiday resorts and secondly as places to retire. This meant that there was no heavy industry or indeed not much industry at all. Generally, the only industries that were not tourist related were the essential services. However in the holiday coast area, there was one notable exception to this, the town of Llandudno Junction. 'The Junction' as it is known, grew up around the railway junction for Llandudno and the Conwy Valley and the station gave the town its name. There were many industries and opportunities for employment here, the railway, the Crosville and the Hotpoint washing machine factory being the principal employers. There was also a bakery, a brickworks and a wholesale trader and other employers. The decline of the transport systems from the mid 1960s onwards had an effect on Llandudno Junction. The end of the steam train era meant the locomotive sheds closed in 1966. The economies brought into effect by the Crosville particularly the abolition of conductors and the drivers taking the fares meant a 50% reduction in employment. Also in 1971 as services reduced, the Llandudno Town depot closed and the all buses and drivers were transferred to Llandudno Junction. At the end of the twentieth century, the Hotpoint factory closed, which was a major blow to the area. Meanwhile, the seaside towns which had never had any industries were beginning to set up small industrial estates as they could no longer survive on tourism alone. Visitors to Llandudno Junction might well be puzzled by the road which links the town with the A55 being named Ffordd / 6G / Road. The road passes what was the location of the Junction loco shed whose code was 6G. So the memory of those days is very much alive to the people who knew the Junction in steam train days.

Chapter 9
THE DECLINE

Tourism experienced a boom in the 1950s. This was seen as being like the old times, like the 1910s and 1920s when the seaside towns were at their busiest, but in reality the decline had already begun. It can be said that the decline began in the 1930s. These were the times of economic depression and fewer people were taking holidays. However as the decade went on and with World War 2 approaching, people were determined they would enjoy themselves and the summer season of 1939 was a busy one and then when war was declared in September of that year all entertainments ceased and that was for a while the end of the towns as seaside resorts. However, as the North Wales coast was considered a safe area, the resorts took in many evacuees, mostly from Liverpool, and also the Ministry of Food was transferred to Colwyn Bay which meant that many hotels and guest houses were converted to government offices. Vast numbers of civil servants came to the town and this enabled Colwyn Bay's six cinemas and repertory theatre to remain open as well as entertainment at the pier pavillion. The BBC transferred its Entertainment Department from London to Bangor and many of the shows were broadcast live from Bangor and from Llandudno. The cinemas in the holiday towns were full every night and so were the buses, trams and trains. The increase in population due to the civil servants certainly enabled all the cinemas and places of entertainment to thrive.

When the war ended and the civil servants went back to London and the service personnel returned home, the towns were very different. For example in Colwyn Bay, the local population were now unable to support six cinemas and even in the summer they were no longer full. The seaside towns began to think for the first time that maybe they would need to earn their living in other ways in addition to tourism.

As we look at the coastal towns in 1950, we nevertheless find a tourist boom. People were starting to spend money again and although wages were low, bus and train fares were cheap and so were hotels and guest houses. Many hotels taken over by civil servants during the war, did not revert to hotel use afterwards. In reality the number of holiday makers visiting the towns was falling and so in the midst of the great post war tourist boom the decline had started. It is in this period that we see the transport systems beginning to decline, slowly at first but later more quickly. The first sign that the railways were cutting back was the closure of Old Colwyn station in 1952. Llanddulas station closed at the same time. In 1954 the pier at Rhos-on-sea was demolished. Next to go was the Llandudno to Colwyn Bay tramway which went in 1956. The tramway had cut the line back from Old Colwyn to Colwyn Bay in 1930. Use of the tramway was decreasing and by the mid 1950s it was running at a loss. By 1961 the buses that replaced the trams ceased. Some cinemas began to close in the 1950s. From the early 1960s onwards, the decline accelerated . The Liverpool & North Wales Steamship company operated its last sailings in 1962 and the following year went into liquidation. From the mid 1960s onwards bus services were reduced. All these things were a sign that holiday habits were changing rapidly and so too was the social structure of society. As car ownership increased and roads were improved it became possible for people to travel from the conurbations of Merseyside, Manchester and Birmingham to North Wales and to return on the same day. As a result the home based B & B businesses collapsed. Also some hotels and guest houses closed. This in turn had an effect on rail and bus services and from the mid 1960s onwards the services began to be reduced. People were now looking further afield for their main annual holiday. This in turn reduced the number of people visiting the North Wales coast. Although car ownership meant greater numbers of people came to North Wales for the day, road congestion had become a major problem by the 1960s. Long traffic queues built up on the approaches to Conwy, at times reaching two miles in length. As well as causing inconvenience to motorists, this played havoc with bus schedules and it was not unusual in the late afternoon and early evening for buses on the Caernarfon - Llandudno route to be up to two hours late. It had been thought that when the 'new' Conwy bridge was built in 1958 that this would solve the traffic problems as traffic would no longer have to queue to get over the one way suspension bridge and pay the toll. The traffic congestion, however, got worse. The next attempt to solve the problem was to build a flyover at Llandudno Junction to avoid the delays to road traffic at the level crossing. A flyover was built, but still this did not solve the problem. Eventually, it was realised that the traffic congestion problem would never be solved until through traffic was cleared from the narrow streets of Conwy. Conwy became a place to avoid and this had a detrimental effect on retail businesses in the town. Colwyn Bay also experienced major problems with traffic congestion on the A55 which ran through the town centre and this virtually brought the town to a standstill. To travel the one mile between Old Colwyn and Colwyn Bay it was quicker to walk than to go by car or bus. Llandudno was more fortunate as no main trunk road ran through the town but even there traffic was getting much heavier and parking had become a major problem. Rhyl and Prestatyn did not have the same problems as Colwyn Bay and Conwy but nevertheless the roads there also got busier. By the late 1960s it was realised that the whole area needed a major revamp of its road system as the car had become a victim of its own success. A report entitled 'The Collcon Report' announced its findings and suggestions and was received with a mixed reception. The two most controversial proposals were a new expressway running through Colwyn Bay, parallel to the railway and a bridge over the Conwy estuary to carry the new expressway. A group was formed in Colwyn Bay under the name 'Save our Seaside' and conservation groups and environmentalists fought against the proposal to bridge the Conwy Estuary. The conclusion was that the Colwyn Bay by-pass was built as planned but the Conwy river was crossed by a tunnel. The new road system in the area was part of the overall plan for a new A55 expressway from Chester to Holyhead. This was built in stages and was completed at the start of this century with the new road across Anglesey.

The new road sent worrying messages to public transport, particularly to the railway. How could the railway now compete with this fast road? Was the decline in public transport to be accelerated? There were fears around this time for the future of the North Wales coast railway. It was feared it may terminate at Llandudno Junction or at Rhyl as a branch line from Chester. Questions were asked as to how the seaside resorts would respond to the new road? Would it bring more people to visit the resorts or would they simply pass them by and leave them deserted? I have in this book considered the development of transport, particularly public transport on the North Wales coast. We have seen the horse rider give way to the stagecoach; the stagecoach give way to the steamer; the steamer give way the railways. By the late twentieth century, many were asking is the railway now giving way to the car? People were also asking will the decline in staying guests and day visitors be halted or will people desert the North Wales resorts in favour of holidays in warmer locations abroad? In the next chapter I will consider this.

Chapter 10

LATER DEVELOPMENT AND THE FUTURE

My main reason for writing the little book has been to record the rise and decline of transport systems on the North Wales coast, but it is far from a simple task to say when the decline began, or indeed if it was a decline at all. History has shown that declines lead to new beginnings. The decline of the stagecoach era meant the beginning of the railway era. The railway began to decline as early as the 1920s when cars were made in large numbers. As the railways brought about mass tourism, this also declined as tourism to the seaside declined.

Let us then look at the situation at the beginning of this century with the new A55 road complete and the effect it has had on the coastal towns. It has brought many benefits to Conwy. People now go there rather than avoid it, and the town is now very popular with tourists. This is probably because this old medieval town has retained its atmosphere at the same time as catering for the modern tourist. More people are now visiting Conwy by car, by bus and by train than for some years. Colwyn Bay has not been so fortunate with many of the former guest houses converted to other uses. Many shops in the town are closed. On the positive side, the promenade is popular and people take advantage of the free parking and the refreshment kiosks some of which are open in winter as well as summer. Colwyn Bay Pier is a sad sight and at the time of writing its future is uncertain. There is a twice weekly street market and a weekly farmers' market and on market days both market and shops do better business. So it appears that although the new A55 has brought its benefits, it does not guarantee prosperity for the seaside towns. History has not treated Rhyl kindly and with the Pavillion theatre and the pier long since gone and also the fun fairs gone, the town has seen much change. As in Colwyn Bay, there is difficulty in finding uses for former guest houses. But there are positive signs here too. There are redevelopment plans at the west end and the railway around the Marine Lake still runs.

Llandudno has stood the test of time better than Colwyn Bay and Rhyl and still retains the atmosphere of a Victorian seaside town. But there have been changes here too. There has been much development in out of town shopping centres and many shops at the top end of Mostyn Street have closed. The town continues to be popular as a tourist destination and major shopping centre.

The general reason for the decline in public transport systems from the 50s and 60s onwards was due not only to changes in holiday patterns but also to increased car ownership. In those days, people's way of thinking was 'If you don't have a car, you go by bus or train. If you do have a car you go by car.' From the beginning of the twenty-first century, many people have begun to rethink this attitude particularly for long distance travel. Railway stations have in recent years had to provide more parking space as an increasing number of people are travelling by train. Other factors have influenced this, such as a growing awareness of environmental issues and the ever increasing cost of fuel. So public transport systems have responded to this by providing better services, and free bus passes for the over 60s have helped this too. Just as we saw decline in public transport in the 1960s as a result of social habits of travel and holidays, now we are experiencing a revival of public transport as attitudes to travel are changing. The North Wales coast now has a better bus and train service than it has ever had and most journeys carry a high capacity of passengers. Although some travel on a free pass, there is also a considerable number of fare paying passengers. The future looks encouraging for public transport.

Early revival of public transport

In one sense the revival in public transport began in the post war years, the very time the major transport systems were declining. This may seem somewhat of a paradox but let me explain. It was in the early 1950s that the railway preservation movement came into being. The Talyllyn Railway from Tywyn to Abergynolwyn on the coast of Meirionydd faced threat of closure. It was then run by the Western Region of British Railways. A group of enthusiasts took over and ran the line as a going concern. This was very much the curtain raiser for other developments. The Ffestiniog Railway from Porthmadog to Blaenau Ffestiniog had closed and an enthusiasts group took over in 1954 and started to run trains again, re-opening the line in stages. While the rebuiling was in progress part of the line was flooded by the electricity generating board and the hope to rebuild to Blaenau looked doomed. However after one of the longest legal cases in history the railway won compensation and the line eventually reached Blaenau in 1982 and ran into a new joint station with the terminus of the line from Llandudno, making connections from the north coast to Porthmadog. Similar narrow gauge railways followed suit, the Welshpool and Llanfair railway which had closed to passengers in 1931 and to freight in 1956, was re-opened by enthusiasts in 1963. Next to re-open was the Llanberis Lake Railway, originally built as the Padarn Railway to carry slates from the Dinorwig quarries to Y Felinheli which was named Port Dinorwig. This railway re-opened in 1971 and was extended to Llanberis village in 2003. Another narrow gauge slate carrying railway although it never re-opened is worthy of mention. The Penrhyn Railway was built to carry slate from the Penrhyn Quarry at Bethesda to Port Penrhyn at Bangor. It closed in 1962 and attempts to preserve it at the time were not successful. Two of its locomotives Linda and Blanche were acquired by the Ffestiniog Railway. However all is not lost. A preservation group exists and has begun a programme of restoration for part of the line.

When the Ruabon to Barmouth standard gauge line was closed in 1965, enthusiasts stepped in to run trains again on part of the route. Although the track had been quickly removed, the enthusiasts laid a narrow gauge track for the length of Llyn Tegid (Bala Lake) running from Llanuwchllyn to a terminus about one mile outside Bala, the site of the old Bala Junction station.

Travelling further south we encounter the Vale of Rheidol Railway, a narrow gauge line running between Aberystwyth and Devil's Bridge. This railway, which was run by the Great Western Railway closed in 1939 at the commencement of World War 2 with the intention of re-opening after the war. It re-opened in 1948 as part the now nationalised British Railways. Despite many threats of closure the line survived and when British Railways became known as British Rail, the Vale of Rheidol steam locomotives carried the British Rail logo just as the main line trains did. It was the last steam powered railway owned by British Rail. In 1989 it was sold to a trust who now operate it.

By the late 1960s , the preserved narrow gauge railways were becoming popular tourist attractions and together with the Snowdon Mountain Railway which has always been run commercially, were jointly marketed as The Great Little Trains of Wales. People were coming to North Wales for their holidays with the specific aim of travelling on these newly restored railways.

Special tickets were issued which gave unlimited travel on all of these little railways.

The standard gauge Llangollen Railway is worthy of mention. This, like the Bala Lake Railway runs on the the trackbed of the former Ruabon to Barmouth Railway. Fortunately, although the track had gone, the station at Llangollen remained in situ which enabled a preservation group to step in in 1975. The railway was re-opened from Llangollen in stages and reached Carrog by 1996. The next will be the extension to Corwen. This standard gauge preserved line has become very popular and has proved a worthy addition to the many tourist attractions in Llangollen.

The preserved narrow gauge railways together with the Llangollen Railway are primarily tourist attractions and are not generally seen as a means of getting from A to B. However, they do nevertheless represent a new era for public transport in North Wales.

As these railways have increased in popularity, motorists have been prepared to get out of their cars to experience a trip on a steam train and admire mountain and valley scenery seen at its best from the train. Even as far back as the 1950s and 1960s the coach companies were quick to see the potential of this by running combined coach and narrow gauge railway tours. This made better use of time and for example enabled a tour from Llandudno to Porthmadog travelling out through Bangor and Caernarfon, and boarding the Ffestiniog Railway train to Tan-y-Bwlch, where after a short walk passengers re-joined the coach and returned to Llandudno via Blaenau Ffestiniog and the Conwy Valley. The newest narrow gauge railway in North Wales to re-open is the Welsh Highland Railway. The history of this railway is somewhat complicated and the details have been well documented elsewhere. In brief, this railway came into being from a number of narrow gauge lines and eventually a through line was completed in 1923 from Dinas (a few miles south of Caernarfon) to Porthmadog. The line was never really a financial success and went into receivership in 1927 and closed in 1936. Unlike other closed lines, there were no thoughts of preservation. However, an enthusiasts group was formed in 1964 with the intention of re-opening at least part of the line. This was not achieved until 1980 when a short section was opened at Porthmadog. In the meantime the Ffestiniog Railway after the re-opening of their line to Blaenau were looking for another project. Eventually they bought the northern section of the track and began operating out of a new station at Caernarfon in 1997. Caernarfon had a railway station again after being 27 years without one. The line opened in stages, first to Waunfawr, then Rhyd Ddu, then Beddgelert and then Pont Croesor. Trains are now running on this line from Caernarfon to Porthmadog. This means a journey of 40 miles by narrow gauge steam railway from Caernarfon to Blaenau Ffestiniog.

The story of the preserved and new railways is North Wales is indeed a success story.

The main line trains have also enjoyed some sort of revival in the last few years. Today, the North Wales coast line enjoys a good service and its future looks assured. There is an hourly service from Llandudno to Manchester and an hourly service from Holyhead to Shrewsbury via Wrexham with alternate trains extending at Shrewsbury to Cardiff and Birmingham. These services are operated by Arriva Trains Wales. The service from London to Holyhead is better and faster than it has ever been, with six through trains a day from Euston to North Wales, five of which run through to Holyhead with one terminating at Bangor. Also, by changing at Chester, North Wales passengers have an hourly service to London. An increasing number of passengers is using the train services and people are seeing the advantage of leaving their car at the railway station and using the train for these long journeys.

Bus services too have experienced some kind of a revival in recent years. From the grim days of the 1970s and 80s when services were reduced to a minimum, we are now seeing much better services. Buses from Llandudno to Rhyl now provide a 12 minute service frequency and from Llandudno to Caernarfon, there is a 15 minute frequency. This is a more frequent service than there has ever been on these routes. The buses are well used and during the summer are usually full. Free bus passes for the over 60s help to fill the buses, but many people now use the buses to go to and from work. The buses now serve many housing areas and there are many new services to places which have not previously enjoyed the benefit of a bus service. In recent years, it has been increasingly difficult to find parking places in the towns both in summer and winter. Also, parking has now become expensive.

So even for local journeys into town, more and more people are discovering the advantage of using buses.

Despite the revivial in bus and train services on the North Wales coast, trams and ships have not experienced a revival. It is much more difficult to get these going again, but the Llandudno and Colwyn Bay Tramway Society is certainly keeping alive the memory of the trams, and we can but hope that one day some kind of tram service may operate.

Shipping services do not seem to have a future in the North Wales resorts. This is not because there is no public demand for them, but because the capital cost of building a vessel of any size would be too great. In addition to this, the landing stage at

Llandudno Pier is currently out of use. This leaves Menai Bridge as the only landing stage in North Wales that can accommodate even moderately sized passenger ships. The exception is of course Holyhead where very large fast craft and conventional ferries leave regularly for Ireland. Apart from this, the only water transport that remains is by very small motor boats. A trip is available from Beaumaris Pier to Puffin Island, although no landing is permitted. From Conwy a larger motor boat runs trips from the town's quay to the estuary of the river and for a short distance up river just beyond the bridges. Boating in recent years has been much more for privately owned boats and the development of marinas at Conwy and Deganwy has shown there is a demand for this. In the summer of 2010, a public river taxi was introduced linking Conwy and Deganwy. Although only a very small boat, this is possibly the first true 'ferry' across the river since 1826.

Holiday Patterns and social structures today

The future of the North Wales coast as a holiday destination seems assured, but the very different social structure of society from that of the 1950s means holiday patterns are now very different. In the 1950s and 60s the holiday season was very short and began and ended at precise times, from Whitsun weekend (going back to the days when the ecclesiastical Whitsuntide was a holiday weekend) until the second week in September when all the holiday facilities closed. Now things are very different and the holiday season is virtually all year although of course it gets considerably busier in the summer. Public transport systems have responded to this by providing equally good services in summer and winter. Hotels run early and late holidays for older people. Another change has been with faster means of travel many people travel to the area for weekends at all times of the year. Most working people now have a month's holiday and tend to take their main holiday abroad and their shorter holidays at home. This means more people visiting North Wales. In the last 50 years, the number of tourist attractions in the area has increased considerably and tourism is marketed more than it has ever been. New attractions for tourists are appearing every year and there is more to do for those who visit North Wales on holiday than there has ever been. All the public transport systems have responded to this. People have more leisure time than ever and this is good for tourism. Tourism is now Wales' biggest industry and the population of Wales is increasing. These factors send a sign of hope to public transport. The changing attitude to travel is continuing and many car owners are seeing the advantage of using both car and public transport. Some people are finding that if they live within walking distance of a good bus and train service, that they don't even need a car. All this is of course good for the environment. So the decline of the 1960s appears to have been reversed and now public transport systems are in good heart.

The Future

It is never easy to predict the future. How will people in 50 years time look back on the social structures and holiday patterns of our day? Will they look on the 2010s as a time of prosperity for tourism and public transport? Will they look on it as an Indian summer before another decline? It seems certain that environmental issues will continue to get a high place on the agenda and this is good news for public transport systems.

Will people have as much leisure time in the future? With future plans pointing to pensions being paid at a later age and people having to work longer, it appears that many people will not have as much leisure time. Global economy will in the future affect tourism and transport in the same way as it will affect every other industry. Social structures will no doubt change in the future as they have in the past.

It is certain that if society is to prosper then an efficient transport system is essential. Society began to learn this as early as the time of the Industrial Revolution. Also, history has taught us that tourism and transport and social structures generally all belong together. Public transport, I believe, will have an increasing role to play in the future.

Although the future is difficult, maybe even impossible to predict, it is nevertheless essential to plan for future transport systems. Such plans will need to take into account environmental issues to achieve the most efficient transport system. Global economy and social structures are even more difficult to plan for, than predicted environmental change. Whatever may happen, people will still want to travel for all kinds of reasons and will still want to go on holiday.

The fact that much of Wales is protected by National Parks or Areas of Outstanding Natural Beauty or conservation areas should be sufficient assurance that the reason why people come here on holiday will remain. In many ways the basic needs of the tourist to this part of the world have not changed. They come to see the natural environment of sea, mountain, valley, river, lake, moorland and the towns and villages whose architecture blends (well it usually does!) with the environment where they are located. Transport and tourism will no doubt have peaks and troughs in the future as in the past. It is encouraging to note that most of the trips I have described in this book from the point of view of a tourist family fifty years ago can still be made today.

Besides this, there are many more tourist attractions now than there have ever been before. Although the twenty-first century marketing of tourism is on a global basis, we nevertheless market the same natural beauty as was marketed in a more simple way in the nineteenth century. And as the pioneers of the tourist industry developed the transport systems which were the best that were achievable in the technology of their day, so the future of tourism in this twenty-first century can be achieved by the continuing development of safe, environmentally friendly and efficient transport systems using the best technology available to us in our day. In this way I see that the holiday towns of the North Wales coast and areas of Wales beyond them will continue to attract tourists and will remain pleasant places in which to live.

Appendix 1

A summary of Crosville bus summer services from Llandudno, Colwyn Bay and Rhyl in the summer of 1962.

Service No.	Route	weekday daytime frequency
A1 A2	Rhyl - Holywell - Chester	every 30 mins
A7	Rhyl - Sealand	workpeoples service as required
B29	Rhyl - St. Asaph - Mold	3 per day
M1	Rhyl - Llanrwst	9 per day
M7-M10	Llandudno-Bangor - Caernarfon	every 20 mins
M7	Llandudno - West Shore Lido	7 per day plus extra as required
M11	Llandudno - Fforddlas Bridge	every hour
M11	Llandudno - Eglwysbach	4 per day
M12 P12	Llandudno - Colwyn Bay - Penmaen Hd.	every 10 mins
M13	Llandudno - Colwyn Bay - Rhyl	every 30 mins
M13	Colwyn Bay - Rhyl	every 15 mins
M14	Colwyn Bay - Betws-yn-Rhos	8 per day
M14	Colwyn Bay- Dawn	4 per day Sat only
M17 M18	Llandudno - Colwyn Bay - Llysfaen	every 20 mins
M17	Llandudno - Colwyn Bay	every 10 mins
M19	Llandudno - West Shore Lido	9 per day plus extra as required
M19 M20	Llandudno - Maesdu - Conwy	every 15 mins
M19 M20	Llandudno - Conwy - Llanrwst	every 30 mins
M21	Colwyn Bay - Bryn-y-Maen	every hour
M21	Colwyn Bay - Holland Arms	5 per day Sat only
M21	Colwyn Bay - Llanrwst	1 per day Market Day only
M22	Conwy - Colwyn Bay - Tan Lan	every 15 mins
M24	Colwyn Bay - Fforddlas Bridge	every hour
M24	Colwyn Bay - Eglwysbach	6 per day
M25	Llandudno - Pydew	4 per day
M26	Rhyl - Ffynongroew	every 10 mins
M26	Rhyl - Holywell	4 per hour
M27	Rhyl - Flint	workpeople's service as required
M28	Rhyl - Greenfield	workpeople's service as required
M29	Rhyl - Talacre	2 per day
M30	Rhyl - Gronant	every 30 mina
M31	Rhyl - Maes Gwilym Camp	17 per day
M31 M32	Rhyl - Holywell via Trelawnyd	7 per day

M33	Rhyl - Holywell via Rhewl Mostyn	2 per day Sat only
M34	Rhyl - Trelogan via Prestatyn	4 per day
M35	Rhyl - Prestatyn - Meliden - Dyserth	every 15 mins
M36	Rhyl - Rhuddlan - Dyserth - Meliden	every 15 mins
M37	Rhyl - Meliden via Roundwood	every 30 mins
M38	Rhyl - Cwm	2 per day Fri only
M39	Rhyl - St. George	every 30 mins
M40 M41	Rhyl - Tremeirchion	6 per day
M42 M43	Rhyl - Cefn	5 per day Sat only, 2 Wed
M45	Rhyl - Towyn	every 15 mins to traffic requirments
M45 M46	Rhyl - Abergele	every 10 mins
M45	Rhyl - Abergele Hospital	every 20 mins
M46	Rhyl - Gwrych Castle Entrance	every 20 mins
M46	Rhyl - Gwyrch Castle	freuquent service as required
M47	Rhyl - Borth Cross Roads	14 per day
M47	Rhyl - Abergele	3 per day
M48	Rhyl - Sarn Rug	infrequent Market Day & Sat only
M49	Rhyl - Trellywelyn Road	4 per day
M50	Rhyl - Llansannan	5 per day
M50	Rhyl - Llanfair TH	14 per day
M51	Rhyl - Denbigh	every 30 mins
M51	Rhyl - Ruthin	every hour
M51	Rhyl - Corwen	10 per day
M54	Rhyl - Eryl Hall	2 per day plus extra as required
M79	Rhyl - Point of Ayr Colliery	workpeople's service as required
M80	Rhyl - Point of Ayr Colliery	workpeople' service as required
M81	Rhyl - Penyffordd	5 per day
M83	Rhyl Grosvenor Ave via Grange Rd	21 per day
M84	Rhyl Grosvenor Avenue via Vale Rd	16 per day
M85	Rhyl - Bridgegate Road	6 per day
M86	Rhyl - Cefndy Road	12 per day

M87	Rhyl seafront service	every 10 mins
M88	Rhyl - Botannical Gardens	every 20 mins
M89	Abergele - Rhyl - Prestatyn	every hour
M91	Rhyl Weaverton - Brynhedydd	9 per day extra on Sat
M92	Colwyn Bay - Seafield Road	8 per day
M95	Llandudno Local Service	12 per day
M97 M98	Llandudno - Colwyn Bay - Denbigh	every hour
P1	Colwyn Bay - Llanrwst - Betws-y-coed	3 per day
P2	Llandudno - Conwy Morfa	every hour
P3 P4	Colwyn Bay - Conwy - Bangor	8 per day

Appendix 2

Train departures (up line) from Llandudno, Colwyn Bay and Rhyl on summer
Saturdays in 1951

Llandudno depart	Colwyn Bay depart	Rhyl depart	Destination
....	....	0600	Chester General
....	....	0640	Chester General
0630	0648	0711	Crewe
0708	0726	0752	Birkenhead Woodside
0740	0759	0818	Manchester Exchange
0750	0810	0831	Liverpool Lime Street
....	....	0833	Chester General
0805	0824	0842	Bradford Exchange
....	0841	0856	Manchester Exchange
....	0855	0911	London Euston
....	....	0920	Birmingham New Street
....	....	0925	Chester General
0855	0915	0932	London Euston
0905	0927	0948	London Euston
0925	0945	....	Coventry
....	....	1015	Manchester Exchange
0945	.....:..	....	Manchester Exchange
....	....	1032	Manchester Exchange
0955	1019	1043	Leicester London Road
1015	....	....	Derby Midland
....	1030	1055	Liverpool Lime Street
....	1100	....	Manchester Exchange
....	....	1105	Stoke-on-Trent
1030	....	1119	Manchester Exchange
....	1111	....	Crewe
....	....	1140	Liverpool Lime Street
1055	1115	1148	Liverpool Lime Street
....	....	1205	Sheffeld Midland
1130	1153	....	Sheffield Midland
1145	1207	1226	Newcastle-on-Tyne
....	....	1240	Manchester Victoria
1205	1228	1252	Leeds City South
1220	1245	1306	London Euston
....	1257	....	Liverpool Lime Street
1255	....	1334	Nottingham Midland & Burton

1305	1320	1352	London Euston
1320	1338	1400	Derby Midland
1340	1401	1424	Derby Midland
....	....	1430	Manchester Exchange
1355	1419	1442	Manchester Exchange
....	....	1455	Chester General
1425	1444	1504	Birmingham New Street
....	1500	....	Manchester Exchange
1450	1511	1540	Birmingham New Street
....	1527	1548	Liverpool Lime Street
1525	1543	1606	Leeds City South
1538	1601	1623	Manchester Exchange
....	1642	1709	Birmingham New Street
1640	1707	1734	Chester General
1715	1740	1801	Stoke-on-Trent
1730	1755	1815	Manchester Exchange
....	1805	1826	Manchester Exchange
....	....	1915	Chester General
1920	1940	2002	Chester General
....	1953	2014	Crewe
1945	2003	2029	Chester General
2020	2038	2057	Chester General
....	2141	2205	Birmingham New Street
....	....	2230	Chester General

Appendix 3

Liverpool & North Wales Steamship Company's sailing schedules for the high summer of 1961.

St. Tudno schedule
Daily except Fridays

Liverpool	depart	1045	Menai Bridge	depart	1545
Llandudno	arrive	1305	Llandudno	arrive	1700
Llandudno	depart	1315	Llandudno	depart	1715
Menai Bridge arr		1440	Liverpool	arrive	1940

The St. Tudno did not sail on Fridays.

St. Seiriol schedule

Sundays

Liverpool	depart	1400
Llandudno	arrive	1630
Llandudno	depart	1830
Liverpool	arrive	2100

Thursdays

Llandudno	depart	0930
Liverpool	arrive	1200
Liverpool	depart	1400
Llandudno	arrive	1630
Llandudno	depart	1830
Liverpool	arrive	2100

Mondays

Liverpool	depart	1400
Llandudno	arrive	1630

Fridays

Liverpool	depart	1045
Llandudno	arrive	1305
Llandudno	depart	1315
Menai Bridge arrive		1440
Menai Bridge depart		1545
Llandudno	arrive	1700
Llandudno	depart	1715
Liverpool	arrive	1940

Tuesdays and Wednesdays

Llandudno	depart	1015
Douglas IOM	arrive	1340
Douglas IOM	depart	1630
Llandudno	arrive	2000

The St. Seiriol did not sail on Saturdays

St. Trillo schedule

Sundays and Wednesdays

Menai Bridge	depart	0900
Llandudno	arrive	1030
Llandudno	depart	1045
for Morning Cruise		
Llandudno	arrive	1215
Llandudno	depart	1430
Menai Bridge	arrive	1600
Menai Bridge	depart	1630
Llandudno	arrive	1800
Llandudno	depart	1930
for Afternoon/Evening Cruise		
2000		
Llandudno	arrive	2100

Tuesdays

Menai Bridge	depart	0900
Llandudno	arrive	1030
Llandudno	depart	1045
Menai Bridge	arrive	1215
Menai Bridge	depart	1245
Llandudno	arrive	1415
Llandudno	depart	1445
for Afternoon Cruise		
Llandudno	arrive	1645
Llandudno	depart	1800
	Menai Bridge	arrive

Mondays and Thursdays

Llandudno	depart	1045
Menai Bridge	arrive	1215
Menai Bridge	depart	1245
Llandudno	arrive	1415
Llandudno	depart	1445
for Afternoon Cruise		
Llandudno	arrive	1645
Llandudno	depart	1800
Menai Bridge	arrive	2000

Fridays

Menai Bridge	depart	0900
Llandudno	arrive	1030
Llandudno	depart	1045
for Morning Cruise		
Llandudno	arrive	1215
Llandudno	depart	1430
Menai Bridge	arrive	1600
Menai Bridge	depart	1630
Llandudno	arrive	1800
Menai Bridge	arrive	2000

The St. Trillo did not sail on Saturdays.

Bibliography

Anderson V.R. & Fox G.K. *Chester to Holyhead Railway.* Oxford Publishing 1984.

Banks, John. *The Prestige Series Crosville.* Venture Publications 1982.

Bolger, Paul. *BR Steam Motive Power Depots LMR.* Ian Allan 1981

Carrol John & Roberts Duncan. *Crosville Motor Services Part 1.* Venture Publications 1995

Crosland Talyor W.J. *Crosville, The Sowing & The Harvest,* Littlebury Bros 1948

Crosland Taylor, W.J. *State Owned without Tears.* Littlebury Bros. 1953

Daniels Gerald & Dench Les. *Passengers no More,* Ian Allan. 1964/73/80

Edwards Geoffrey, *Colwyn Bay 1934-1974.* A Social History

Hitches, Mike. *The Irish Mail,* Sutton Publishing 2000

Jones, Ivor Wynne. *Llandudno, Queen of the Welsh Resorts.* John Jones, Cardiff 1975

Jones, Michael. *Steam on the North Wales Coast.* Oxford Publishing. 1996

Roberts, Duncan. *Crosville Motor Services 2.* NBC Books 1997

Roberts, Duncan. *Crosville 3. The Sucessors 1986-2001,* NBC Books 2001.

Rolt L.T.C. *Red for Danger.* Pan Books 1976

Rolt L.T.C *Thomas Telford. Longmans,* Green & Co. 1958.

Shepherd, John. *The Liverpool & North Wales Steamship Company.* Ships in Focus 2006

Thornley, Frank. *Steamers of North Wales.* T.Stevenson, Prescot 1952/62

Tucker, Norman. *Colwyn Bay, Its Origin and Growth.* Colwyn Bay Borough Council 1953.

Tucker, Norman. *Conway and its Story.* Gwasg Gee. 1960

Turner, Keith. *The Great Orme Tramway.* Gwasg Carreg Gwalch, Llanrwst, 2003

Turner, Keith. *The Llandudno & Colwyn Bay Electric Railway.* Oakwood Press. 1993.

Turner, Keith. *North Wales Tramways.* David & Charles 1979.

Walking Books by Christopher Draper

Visit our website for further information:
www.carreg-gwalch.com

Orders can be placed on our
On-line Shop

Further enjoyable reading on History and Heritage

Visit our website for further information:
www.carreg-gwalch.com

Orders can be placed on our
On-line Shop